This book should be returned/renewed by the latest date shown above. Overdue items incur charges which prevent self-service renewals. Please contact the library.

Wandsworth Libraries
24 hour Renewal Hotline
01159 293388
www.wandsworth.gov.uk

Wandsworth

D1422181

9030 00004 4505 2

EDITH BOWMAN'S GREAT BRITISH MUSIC FESTIVALS

BLINK

bringing you closer

Published by Blink Publishing
107-109 The Plaza, 535 King's Road,
Chelsea Harbour, London, SW10 0SZ

www.blinkpublishing.co.uk

facebook.com/blinkpublishing
twitter.com/blinkpublishing

978 1 90582 541 7

A CIP catalogue ~~record for this book is available~~ from the British Library.

Design by Steve Leard
~~steveleard.co.uk~~

Printed and bound by ~~Totem,~~ Poland

1 3 5 7 9 10 8 6 4 2

Papers used by Blink Publishing are natural, recyclable products made from
wood grown in sustainable forests. The manufacturing processes conform to
the environmental regulations of the country of origin.

Blink Publishing is an imprint of the Bonnier Publishing Group
www.bonnierpublishing.co.uk

With all my love Tom, Rudy & Spike xxx

TAKE YOUR FESTIVAL EXPERIENCE BEYOND THE PRINTED PAGE...

Pack up your tent, charge your smartphone and head out into the great unknown with Edith's Great British Music Festivals App! With exclusive interviews featuring the likes of Sir Paul McCartney, Jake Bugg, Sharleen Spiteri and many, many more, find out what really happens backstage and how even the most prestigious musicians kick back at some of their favourite live events of the year. Access the free app from iTunes App Store or Google Play Store, point your device at the pages with the special icon and the interviews will be revealed on the device's screen*. Here you will get the chance to listen to Edith's exclusive interviews with some of the world's most legendary festival acts, as well as access 'Edith's Essentials' for every festival featured in the book.

* Subject to minimum device requirements, please see individual apps for more details.

Edith's Music Festival App requires an internet connection to be downloaded, and can be used on iPhone, iPad or Android devices. For direct links to download the app and further information, visit www.blinkpublishing.co.uk.

INTRODUCTION

Thanks for coming along for the ride. This has been one of the most exciting, nerve-wracking, liberating and fun things I've ever done. When the idea was suggested to write a book on British music festivals it felt like such a natural thing for me to do. I've spent half my life going to them, not just in the UK but all over the world, through work, as a music fan and as the dedicated wife of a musician.

My first festival experience was at T in the Park in 1995 when I was at university in Edinburgh and doing work experience for the local radio station, Forth FM. I was asked to go along as a runner to help out with the live broadcasts that were happening over the weekend. That sense of excitement and anticipation is something that I feel even now on a journey to a festival: the butterflies in the tummy, the tapping foot and sitting up in the car like a child, eager to see what visual stimulus is around. I remember arriving, hearing a distant hum of music being kicked around on the wind, almost pulsating into your psyche. Seeing the visual clues and signs of the site as we got closer – an enormous coloured tent top, a big wheel, armies of music fans marching into battle with camping gear and provisions hanging off their bodies – was unforgettable. The excitement was instantaneous and I couldn't believe that I'd never been to a festival before.

Being at T in the Park with 'work' meant I had free rein and I ran around and saw as much as possible in between doing duties for the radio station. It was the year Kylie Minogue was due to play the main stage and my first mission (and one that I was desperate to fulfil) was to seek her out for an interview. I left our makeshift studio of a black double-decker bus with my little audio recorder and went in search of the little pop princess. To cut a long story short, I clocked her going into the ladies' toilets backstage and, instead of following her in, I just paced around outside, looking slightly suspicious, until she emerged, all smiles and hair. I took a deep breath and introduced myself and asked if I could interview her.

'Sure,' she said. It was a moment of confidence and I have no idea where it came from but I threw myself into it. But my first festival broadcast had begun and I think that is where it all started for me on a personal level. The bands, the atmosphere, and the crowd gathering to watch and experience a variety of performances in an environment like no other – it was glorious. I loved the challenge that a festival threw up, both physically and mentally, from a professional point of view.

If you had asked me then, I would never have imagined that I would go on to experience so many festivals over the years and broadcast them for both TV and radio for BBC, Sky, MTV and Channel 4. I'm a very lucky girl. And we are a very lucky generation; most of us are part of the birth of the age of festivals. We are spoilt for choice: there is something for everyone out there when it comes to music and festivals, for all ages and genres. In doing my research for this book I was amazed but also slightly ashamed there were so many I didn't know about. It would be about four or five times thicker if I mentioned every festival that takes place in Britain throughout the year – something that would actually be impossible to do as many come and go, take a break, or unfortunately disappear, never to be seen again. It's a hugely competitive market and festival organisers can no longer take for granted what has come before – they have to be looking to the future, constantly evolving, sometimes in extremely subtle ways, sometimes with hugely obvious changes and improvements.

There was a time when there were only a few festivals dotted around the UK – namely Glastonbury, Isle of Wight and Reading. In fact, when I spoke to my mum when writing this book, she recalls that going to a music festival was never an option when she was younger – there was nothing going on where she grew up in the East Neuk of Fife and the idea of going down to Glastonbury was never a conversation since they didn't really know that much about it. But that's not to say music wasn't a big part of my local area: folk music has always been popular, rich in talent and never short of singer/songwriters with their guitars, fiddles or boxes (accordions). Kenny Anderson, aka King Creosote, grew up in the same area and I remember as a kid watching him play in his dad's Ceilidh band whilst his sister, Lynn, performed a sword dance. It's so exciting to see how inspiring he has been to others and how successful he has become. I know a lot of people, both musicians and music fans, who thoroughly enjoyed being part of Kenny's festival project 'Homegame' that took place over a number of years in my home town. If only there had been something similar when I was growing up. That said, I vaguely remember a bigger local live music event organised off the back of Live Aid in 1988, in St Andrews, Fife. The line-up wasn't too bad either: Marillion, Go West, Runrig, The Sugarcubes, Rose Royce, Phil Manzanera from the Doors, Jack Bruce and Captain Sensible all made appearances, and there were theatre and dance workshops, art galleries, folk musicians, pipers and poets, face painting, a creche, puppets, magicians, mask making, belly dancing and an amazing fairground! I have no idea why we didn't go, but it would have been a glorious introduction to the festival atmosphere.

What do I love about festivals? Well, this book is the answer to that. Every festival is unique in its own way, and even if you only went to one festival every year for the rest of your life, you would have a different experience every year. I guess it's the unknown-ness that's appealing – you put your confidence in the festival and if you allow yourself to be fully immersed then it can be life changing, or at least create memories you will cherish for the rest of your life. Festivals are not just about the music, it's about the shared experience and being with friends or partners. I've been so incredibly lucky to see the most powerful and evocative performances, from a favourite artist for the first time or seeing a band for the 100th time (both are allowed!), but when I think of festivals I think of the people I was with first, then the music.

One of the hardest things in putting this guide together was deciding on which festivals to write about. I began by looking at the festivals that I know best – the ones that I have years of experience attending in various capacities. Then it was time to learn about some new ones and widen my festival-attending routine. That was the fun bit as I found myself heading to a number of festivals on my own and what a wonderfully enriching experience that was. Just me and my camera, wandering free. If I ever go missing, the corner of a festival site might be the first place to look for me!

My festival attendance has been a mixture of business and pleasure, but even with the business side of things, there is always pleasure. Working at Glastonbury, Reading and Leeds, One Big Weekend, Latitude, V and T in the Park over the years has been one of my favourite jobs ever and I never dreamt it would be something I would actually be able to achieve. I remember those first years at T with Forth FM, watching the

STV presenters and thinking to myself, I want to be doing that job. I'm now doing exactly that and it has given me some of the most memorable working experiences ever! I've also had the pleasure of working with brilliant people on camera – Zane Lowe, Colin Murray, Reggie Yates and Greg James – and then on Channel 4 with Cat Deeley, Vernon Kay and Steve Jones. You can't be working at a festival and just do the job (well I can't); you have to look for those hours of downtime as the perfect, and sometimes only, opportunity to watch bands and explore. When I'm working at Glastonbury for the BBC, I am normally on air until around midnight, so that's when I get the chance to head off and explore. I also get the opportunity to catch some bands during the day, particularly if I'm on site a few hours before I begin work.

In the first few years Colin Murray and I broadcast from Glastonbury, we stayed in a tiny little caravan just behind the Pyramid Stage in the BBC compound, and there wasn't anyone to keep an eye on us or escort us off site to get a good night's sleep (in fact I'm not sure we slept at all!). There was nothing better than waking up to the soundcheck on the Pyramid Stage for the day ahead – my idea of the perfect alarm call! I'm sure our, shall we say, 'enthusiasm', for the festival was one of the reasons we were then moved to a bed and breakfast up the road in Street in the subsequent years, probably so they could keep an eye on us.

The bed and breakfast accommodation, I have to say, was a very welcome retreat in 2008 when I was working at the festival two weeks after I'd had my first child, Rudy, with a c-section! The journey down there from London with the car packed with so much stuff (including a small fridge to store my breast milk) was a bit of a daze. My husband Tom was playing a warm-up show with his band Editors that night ahead of their Glastonbury appearance the following day, so we were on a pretty tight time frame. It was Rudy's first big car journey and I'll be honest, not his best! To say I was a bit delirious by the time we got there would be an understatement. Once everything was in our room, including my mum who had come to help out over the weekend, Tom turned to me and said, 'Don't worry, we've done the right thing, it's all going to be fine. This little person has come into our life and we are showing him our world.' Those words were all I needed to hear for confirmation that we weren't mental for going to a festival two weeks after having a baby. First thing the next morning it was time to get on site and start work and broadcast live on TV. A few hours into our broadcast I vividly remember enquiring with our producer, Sally, about the duration of the next live performance, and how long I had before I was back on camera.

'About 15 minutes,' was her reply.

'I'll be back in nine,' I said.

I then hobbled down from the treehouse studio to our allotted Portakabin and proceeded to express milk for about eight minutes. I popped the milk in a little fridge I had brought with me for that exact reason, and shuffled back upstairs and back on set ready for more live TV. Crazy, you may think, but looking back now I wouldn't (and couldn't) have done it any other way!

Going to a festival and not working is a very different experience, particularly when your husband is also one of the performers – but I'm normally the first off the tour bus with my camera, darting around taking pictures of this and that. This is something that I'm really happy to share with you in this book – a little collection of my personal festival pictures. It's something I've been doing for a few years now – taking full advantage of my access to snap away. Up until now I've been quite nervous and shy about showing people, but with encouragement from friends and the people in some of the photos, I've decided to share them with you. I hope you like them.

I've been to at least three festivals every year since that first year at T. I'm pretty proud of that and I hope that never changes. In fact I now have the opportunity to take my own small people to them! Rudy, who is seven in the summer of 2015, has already been to Latitude twice, Hop Farm, Bestival, Camp Bestival, V, Reading and Glastonbury four times. And that's just the UK Festivals.

I didn't want to overload this book with personal experiences – listing bands I've seen, talking about the weather a lot, and generally gushing about everything. I wanted it to be a companion, a bit like a friend who has been to the festival before and can guide you through the basics, and encourage you to have your own adventure. I have included some stories and in doing so was reminded of how jammy I've been to have attended so many amazing festivals over the years. Looking back at my pictures has been a way of igniting memories that have been neglected; they make me smile relentlessly from the inside out. I want you to learn something about each festival, whether you've been or not, including its history, the music, the people and how it's changed over the years, or simply why it began. That's also why I've included a brilliant little digital app, which features a whole load of extra content for your eyes and ears. I reached out to people I've been lucky enough to get to know over the years and managed to get some time with some of them to chat about their experiences. From Damon Albarn's discussion on how festival appearances can be paramount to a band's career, to what happened to Coldplay's Will Champion when he first visited Reading back in the 1990s, the app will get you closer to the festival experience and shed even more light on the Great British music festival circuit.

Finally, the UK festival scene has begun to truly flourish over the past decade. So much so that UK festivals are now some of the most internationally-renowned in the world, with festival goers from all corners of the globe returning to some of the British Isle's greatest parties. And for so many festivals now it's not just about the music – the significance of which, unlike previous decades, has receded slightly over the years – these cultural behemoths now include a wide range of international art forms and cater for the broadest possible spectrum of people. The bottom line is about providing for the audience to ensure they have the best time possible – and all the festivals included in this book are a testament to doing just that.

This book would not have been possible without the help of a huge number of generous, kind, funny and honest people. First to everyone at Blink for suggesting the idea and in particular my fabulous editor Joel Simons. Also in no particular order: Noel Gallagher, Lily Allen, Tom and Serge from Kasabian, Sharleen Spiteri, Jake Bugg, Sam and Ross from Twin Atlantic, Will from Coldplay, Arlene Moon, Phil Harvey, Damon Albarn, Bobby Gillespie, Sir Paul McCartney, Stuart Bell, Nicola Martin, Simon Young, Nan Davies, Thomas Coxhead, Huw Stevens, Andy Copping, Becci Abbot, Will Cook, Melvin Benn, Douglas Anderson, Stuart from Mogwai, Mark Radcliffe, Geoff Ellis, Luke Bainbridge, Lucy Flynn, and Rob Da Bank. I'd also like to thank Francis, Caroline and Megan at Money Management; Nathan, Pandora and Nancy at Public Eye; and Sam Sewell, Biffy Clyro, Neil Anderson, Keith Armstrong, Justine Ward, Hayley Absalom, Charly Hutchings, Niamh Byrne and Barry Hogan from ATP. Thanks too to all the bands, tour managers, PAs and pluggers who have let me take pictures over the years. All the artists that kindly said 'yes' to being interviewed, some of whom are in this book in spirit as we just couldn't synchronise time. Thank you to my family, in particular Mum, Dad, my brother Alex, and Nicola and Kerr and Hallie. Nanny Helen I couldn't have done it without your help and thanks to my dear, dear friends for being so patient with me. I look forward to now seeing more of you!

*One of my favourite
ever pictures –
Florence at Radio 1's
Big Weekend.*

RADIO 1'S BIG WEEKEND

WHERE: *Various locations* **WHEN:** *End of May*

RADIO 1'S BIG WEEKEND
Most likely to see:
Everything you hear on the station.

SCAN HERE

Scan here to see Edith's
Big Weekend essentials.

One of my earliest childhood memories was going to the Radio 1 Roadshow on Portobello Beach. My only live music experience up until then was when my mum dragged me to two Rod Stewart concerts to feed her obsession with the great man (I saw him twice before the age of ten!). But all I can remember about the Roadshow was that it seemed like thousands of freezing kids had turned up on a long stretch of damp, sandy beach, desperate to get a glimpse of Big Fun, miming on the roof of what looked like an articulated lorry. T-shirts were like gold dust and you were buzzing if you managed to grapple a pen from the thousands thrown from the roof (and don't get me started on whether I got a double-sided car sticker or not!). Little did I know that ten years later I would have the opportunity to be part of the next stage in the Radio 1 Roadshow, what is now known as the Big Weekend.

THE RADIO 1 ROADSHOW – A PERSONAL HISTORY

When I joined Radio 1 in 2003 Colin Murray and I were hosting the weekend morning show where we were young scallywags who had a real passion for music and didn't really like being told what to do. We fought to get records played that we really believed in and pushed the boundaries as far as we could without losing our jobs. It was a golden time for me: I was finally submerged in the world I'd looked on from afar. I had the responsibility of playing records to people and I loved, and still do, every second of it. I also had the opportunity to get involved with the live shows put on by the station and to continue the long tradition of broadcasting live music at the BBC.

From the thousands of John Peel sessions, through to the legendary Maida Vale gigs, Radio 1 has always been a champion of live music and bringing live music to the people. Its wonderful live music heritage began with its annual summer roadshows, which ran from the 1970s through to the 1990s. The shows used to take up the entire summer holidays – from July for eight weeks – broadcasting from 10am to 12:30pm each weekday from a beach resort or location around the UK. The original idea came from Johnny Beerling, a BBC

Serge from Kasabian rocks the main stage at the Radio 1 Big Weekend.

'FROM THE THOUSANDS OF JOHN PEEL SESSIONS, THROUGH TO THE LEGENDARY MAIDA VALE GIGS, RADIO 1 HAS ALWAYS BEEN A CHAMPION OF LIVE MUSIC AND BRINGING LIVE MUSIC TO THE PEOPLE.'

Rita Ora performs at Radio 1's Big Weekend. I think it was her debut but she looked as if she'd been doing it all her life!

producer who went on to become the Controller of Radio 1. The first roadshow was held in 1973 in Newquay and was hosted by Alan Freeman from a caravan with a drop down stage. By the mid-1990s, the BBC was broadcasting at 54 live dates over nine weeks from a very impressive stage. The largest was held at Sutton Park in Birmingham in 1992 in celebration of 25 years of Radio 1 – with the likes of Del Amitri, Aswad, The Farm and Status Quo rocking the stage in front of 100,000 fans. The Quo were particularly ripe for a game of 'Bits and Pieces' – the classic, simple and downright legendary game which allowed the live audience (and those watching at home) to play along with the musicians live on stage at the roadshow. The game ran for years and every so often it gets to show its face once again!

The final 'roadshow' took place in Manchester at Heaton Park in 1999 and the following year saw the start of 'One Big Sunday', a series of one-day pop events every Sunday during July and August. Come 2003 it had once again evolved, this time into 'One Big Weekend', which for the next two years happened twice a year in April and then September in Manchester, Cardiff, Derry and Londonderry, and Birmingham. This was the start of the transformation from one-off roadshow events to proper, weekend-long festivals. Radio 1 had the power and punch to stand up amongst the big guns and pull in a line-up to envy its competitors – namely the commercial stations. The White Stripes, Pink, Travis, Badly Drawn Boy, Dido, Basement Jaxx, Ash, Chemical Brothers, The Streets, Keane, Franz Ferdinand, Kasabian and Goldie Looking Chain were just some of the names that played over those two years – names with a mix of worldwide success and huge potential.

In May 2005 the events were reduced to one a year but increased in size to 30,000 over a Saturday and a Sunday. The first of these took place in Herrington Country Park in Sunderland with Foo Fighters, KT Tunstall, Gwen Stefani and The Futureheads amongst the line up. One of my lasting memories of this event was the freakish biblical-like weather that we experienced – hailstones so loud that on one particular afternoon they almost drowned out the sound of the band playing in the tent as they crashed onto the big top with such immense force. I'd never seen weather like it, and I'm Scottish! Next it was on to Dundee and to Camperdown Park, where I had, in fact, spent many a school trip whilst a nipper just across the Tay in Fife (more on Dundee later!). In 2007 the Weekender moved on to Moor Park in Preston followed by Mote Park in Maidstone where Madonna arrived by chopper and Fat Boy Slim headlined the outdoor stage. The thing about having such a big name as Madonna taking part in one of these events, where normally everyone is swanning around sharing hair straighteners and throat sweets, was that she imposed an element of military security around her compound. Everyone was a little bit scared of being within five feet of her wall of bodyguards (not that we could even get anywhere close to five feet of her anyway – I was too busy watching my other half nail it with Editors as they headlined the 'In New Music We Trust' stage).

Swindon hosted the show in 2009 with Snow Patrol, Lily Allen and The Prodigy among the line-up. That year also saw the launch of the BBC Introducing stage, a showcase for new and unsigned artists. Introducing is now part of the furniture, thankfully, a BBC initiative that runs across stations, networks and regions to provide an opportunity for new and unsigned artists to get their music heard by a larger audience and push them towards bigger and better things. In 2004 Bombay Bicycle Club, Wretch 32 and Marina and the Diamonds played for the first time. I remember very clearly how nervous and hungry a young Bombay Bicycle Club were; I was lucky enough to do possibly their first ever interview backstage

just before they performed and lead singer Jack Steadman was almost mute in the interview. Later that

'THE BBC INTRODUCING STAGE IS NOW PART OF THE FURNITURE, THANKFULLY, A BBC INITIATIVE THAT RUNS ACROSS STATIONS, NETWORKS AND REGIONS TO PROVIDE AN OPPORTUNITY FOR NEW AND UNSIGNED ARTISTS TO GET THEIR MUSIC HEARD...'

summer I proudly watched them play Glastonbury just after their debut album, *I Had The Blues But I Shook Them Loose*, was released, and even in that short space of time the confidence, drive and talent shone through in abundance – it was clear they were destined for bigger slots.

Then it was on to Wales in 2005 and the stunning setting (and weather) of Faenol Estate near Bangor. This was an incredible year, which saw Florence and the Machine take centre stage along with the utterly brilliant Biffy Clyro, Cheryl Cole, JLS and Jared Leto and 30 Seconds to Mars! Joy Formidable were the band to come through BBC Introducing that year.

One of my lasting memories of the 2011 edition at Carlisle Airport was DJing with Nick Grimshaw just

The heavens are about to open... but at least we have our tents!

before The Strokes headlined on the 'In New Music We Trust' Stage; only a few hours later someone called

'THE WEEKENDER IS NOW A MAINSTAY OF THE MUSIC CALENDAR AND AN EVENT THAT SHOWCASES UP AND COMING BANDS AND ARTISTS AS WELL AS MORE ESTABLISHED HEADLINERS.'

'Lady Gaga' performed and arrived on stage in a coffin – I will say no more! Another great memory is being on the train with some of my Radio 1 colleagues, flicking through social media and a collection of magazines bought for the journey: I offered to do a shop run to stock up on supplies, only to find on my way to the buffet car a couple of Arctic Monkeys – not the normal passengers you expect on the way to Carlisle – and they weren't even on the bill... Or were they? An alternative mode of transport might have been a better idea to keep the 'secret guests' a secret a little longer. Nevertheless it was always a pleasure and never a chore to catch up with Mr Turner who was on his usual spirited form.

In 2012 London hosted the

Olympics and Hackney Marshes hosted the renamed 'Radio1's Big Weekend', and what a show to coincide with the Olympics next door: Jay Z and Rihanna topped the bill and brought down the curtain on a festival that hosted more stages and a bigger crowd than ever before.

RADIO 1'S BIG WEEKEND TODAY

The event in Hackney pretty much set the bar for all subsequent 'Big Weekends'. Suddenly Radio 1 was up there with the big guns and heralding the start of the festival season with its annual event in May. The Big Weekend is now a mainstay of the music calendar and an event that showcases up and coming bands and artists as well as more established headliners. Some people might argue it's not really a festival but I think over the years Radio 1 has put in the groundwork and proved it can offer something different to what else is on offer. Yes it's based around pop, it's based around charts and it's based around their playlist; but if you list the bands that have played the event over the years and look at the bands that have been supported, you have to hand it to Radio 1 – it knows how to put on and maintain a quality festival. Plus it has endless broadcasting capabilities: I think only Glastonbury gets more coverage on TV, radio, online, social media and in the press.

THE PEOPLE OF THE BIG WEEKEND

Left: Savages take to the BBC Introducing Stage at Radio 1's Big Weekend. It was the first time I had seen them and was hooked. Jehnny Beth is amazing live.

Perhaps the biggest hurdle for the Big Weekend's organisers is making the ticket allocation spread as geographically fair as possible. When the festival began, the organisers set up ticket giveaways around the venue and it was a case of first come first served; but even the BBC were surprised by how far people would travel to get tickets, so it didn't always work out that way. An online ticketing system was introduced in 2006 for two reasons: to distribute the tickets more evenly across local residents and to combat free tickets being sold on online auctions (it's the biggest free ticketed event in Europe, after all!).

The type of people that go to the festival are quite obviously Radio 1 listeners, although that's not an easy demographic to put your finger on – they vary in age, sex, and musical interests. As much as Radio 1 would like to see thousands of 16-24 year olds fill its arenas every year, they can't completely alienate those outside that demographic. You know what to expect when you go along

to a Big Weekend; you know what kind of experience you are going to have. You might have watched it before or you might have heard it on the radio before. It does as it says on the tin and it doesn't really have an opportunity to expand on those expectations in a way that say Glastonbury or Latitude does. That's probably down to the way the site is set out and the fact you can only attend for a day.

When we took the event to Dundee back in 2006 I felt like a proud relative for both the event and the crowd. I was so happy that the BBC had chosen Dundee; it's a city that isn't given the time of day. Edinburgh and Glasgow, then probably Aberdeen, would probably be first choice well before Dundee when it comes to anything on a scale like the Big Weekend. But that is what the event had been trying to do over the previous few years – hit those places just outside the big cities and give them something they will never forget. Dundee certainly didn't forget and to this day, almost ten years later, I still get people telling me it was the best weekend of their lives. And that audience could not have shown their appreciation any more than they did over that weekend. Now I've experienced incredible Scottish crowds over the years but there was something quite magical and euphoric about the atmosphere in those tents. Particularly when

Lily Allen entertains
the crowd on stage
as usual.

the surprise guests were revealed to be Franz Ferdinand, who almost took the roof off the afternoon slot with a blistering set that included 'Take Me Out' and 'Do You Want To', amongst many others.

I also had to turn my phone off a good week leading up to the event as I'm not sure there were any more tickets remaining for the countless friends and relatives who asked for a few.

THE MUSIC

The music at the festival can't really veer too far away from what the mainstream DJs are playing – that, after all, is what the listeners want to come and hear. That said, Radio 1's Big Weekend has always managed to impress with the line-up: it has never failed to grab a great headliner or the odd surprise guest, and with the additions of the BBC Introducing Stage showcasing new and emerging talent, and the 'In New Music We Trust' Stage providing an eclectic alternative line-up for the Radio 1 listeners, the festival's reach is truly far and wide. The main stage does what it is supposed to do, by providing a cross section of the bands and artists you hear every day on the station. Meanwhile, the Outdoor Stage does one of two things: it hosts 'versus' battles, a contest between a few 'superstar' DJs and the BBC's very own songsters (for example, Zane Lowe versus Mark Ronson – now that is one hell of a DJ battle! Zane would start the mix, then Mark plays the next track and it goes back and forward, with the obligatory crowd banter to keep them involved and entertained!). The other purpose of the Outdoor Stage is to keep the party going that little bit longer – it continues for

'NO OTHER FESTIVAL HAS A DIFFERENT LOCATION EVERY YEAR THAT WILL SPECIFICALLY TAILOR ITS STRUCTURE AND FRAMEWORK AROUND THE MUSICAL TASTES AND POPULARITY OF ITS AUDIENCE.'

a good while after the main stage and 'In New Music We Trust' Stage have closed.

Every year something new is either added or tried out – the organisers never seem to be settled with what has gone before, even when what has gone before has been hugely successful. Take the Glasgow edition in 2014, where for the first time two sites in the same city were used – Glasgow Green for the main two-day event and George Square for the Opening Party. The Big Weekend saw the city centre transformed into an outdoor rave, with DJs such as Tiesto, Martin Garrix, Pete Tong and Annie Mac cracking out the tunes to a euphoric crowd of 14,000 people with a backdrop 3D projection kissing the surrounding city buildings.

In fact one of the festival's greatest assets is its ability to tailor itself to the variety of its audience. Glasgow is another great example of a location and population that has a real passion for its music and a place where dance music culture is a huge pull. So a specific dance event was introduced in George Square, right in the centre of Glasgow, both the weekend before The Big Weekend and the night before it all started in Glasgow Green. That would not have worked in every location but for Glasgow it was unique and the right thing to do.

Only Tom from Kasabian could get away with those glasses!

Florence does her thing.

A BIG FESTIVAL FOR A BIG WEEKEND

The Radio 1 Big Weekend is a one off, even though it happens every year. No other festival has a different location every year that will specifically tailor its structure and framework around the musical tastes and popularity of its audience. It's free, apart from the booking fee, and it's probably the only festival you are likely to see One Direction play at. In fact it might be the only festival One Direction have ever played at. Some may argue that it's not really a festival – that it is just an extension of what they did all those years ago, a souped up modern version of the roadshow. But for all the Big Weekends I've been part of, I'm still looking for a double-sided car sticker!

AC/DC performed a legendary set at Download in 2010.

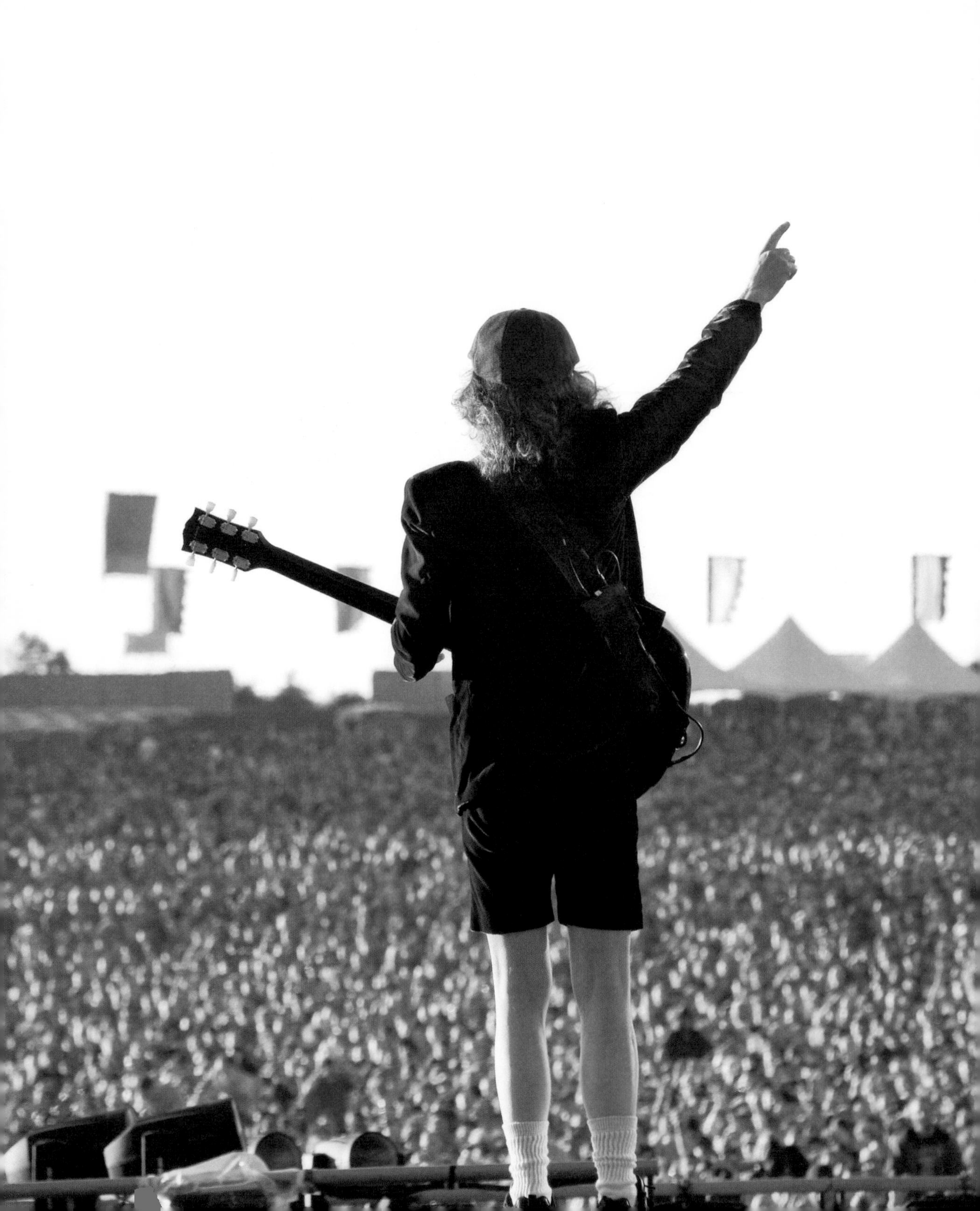

DOWN LOAD

WHERE: *Leicestershire*   **WHEN:** *First two weeks of June*

DOWNLOAD
Most likely to see: A goth or a gimp mask.
Or maybe a goth in a gimp mask!

Scan here to see Edith's
Download essentials.

Download Festival is a bit like the mythological phoenix – rising from the flames, growing like a regenerated rock god, reincarnated from the ash of Monsters of Rock to what it is today. A metal festival, a punk festival and a classic rock festival: it's all those and more – even with a dash of pop! It's a rock festival that incorporates so many genres into its warm and affectionate arms, many of which involve guitars – my favourite! Even the location – Castle Donington – has an air of gravitas to it, as if it might be a location for a *Lord of the Rings* battle. Its diversity is impeccable, especially for a genre-specific festival, and its history and tradition set the foundations of respect and expectation that continues today.

Download Festival is the festival that will surprise you the most, particularly if you're a festival virgin. You might think you know what the festival is all about – the bands, the people, the site and the atmosphere – but even the seasoned Download Festival goer should be prepared to be astonished.

'A METAL FESTIVAL, A PUNK FESTIVAL AND A CLASSIC ROCK FESTIVAL: IT'S ALL THOSE AND MORE...'

A REGENERATED ROCK GOD

The first Download Festival was in 2003, spread over two days and across two stages. But the essence of the festival really began back in 1980 with 'Monsters of Rock', originally a one-day event that attracted an audience of 35,000 heavy metal fans. Over the next 15 years the festival grew to over 100,000 punters and also helped cement the Midlands as the home of heavy metal (although Ozzy Osbourne might also have had something to do with that!).

It proved so successful that the brand went global, popping up in West Germany, Sweden, France, Italy, Spain, USSR, Poland, Belgium, Hungary and all the way to Chile, Argentina and Brazil. As a genre-festival, though, Monsters of Rock became a victim of the natural cycle of music, and the decline in interest corresponded with a few high-profile cancellations in the early 1990s. Even big name headliners such as Metallica, Ozzy Osbourne

*Japanese industrial
metal group
Crossfaith take to
the stage at 2014's
Download.*

and Kiss in the subsequent years couldn't save the inevitable and the festival was eventually cancelled in 1997.

Yet the spirit of Donington Park refused to die. It was, after all, a wonderful live music location and a site that had housed music events for over 25 years. The site, a motorsport circuit near Castle Donington, lies where the three counties of Nottinghamshire, Leicestershire and Derbyshire meet, offering perfect transportation to the site from all over the country. It had everything needed to run a music festival: the infrastructure, the aesthetic, the location – so it came as no surprise that music promoters Andy Copping and Stuart Galbraith jumped at the chance to host their brand new festival on the site. It simply needed to be updated and refreshed – with newer bands, multiple stages and, of course, camping – but the all-

important foundations of Download were already in place.

But why the name 'Download'? It certainly is very unusual, given its current association with disposable pop and the continuous tug of war between artists and the internet. Its origins, however, are a lot more organic: Andy Copping, the festival's co-founder, ran a competition in the office for people to come up with a name for the new festival and offered a £200 prize to the winner. 'Lots of different suggestions were made but everyone seemed to really like "Download",' he recalls. 'It just had a ring to it. Interestingly this was just before the age of downloading music became the norm. So when that was spawned we luckily had a name that was relating itself to music and was always on people's lips.'

The first event, spanning across two days, took place in 2003 and it picked up *Kerrang* magazine's

'event of the year' award, but all the subsequent editions – from 2005 – have been spread across the conventional three-day format. Iron Maiden were the first band to headline the main stage for its maiden edition, topping a Saturday night bill that included Marilyn Manson, Deftones and Funeral for a Friend. Audioslave headed the Sunday night after The Darkness, Evanescence and Billy Corgan's Zwan had suitably warmed up the crowd throughout the day. Subsequent headliners have included: Linkin Park, Pennywise, more Iron Maiden, Korn, Kiss, Metallica, Billy Idol, Black Sabbath, System of a Down, Motorhead and Guns 'N' Roses. It truly is a haven for rock lovers of all ages.

Rob Zombie entertains the crowd at the main stage in 2014.

DOWNLOAD TODAY

The original aim of the festival was to create a community and to become the biggest rock festival in the world. As of today it's the second biggest festival in the UK with an audience of over 110,000. For good reason, too: Download breeds headliners – its organisers take huge risks by elevating bands to a slot that may appear to be over their head, but which normally turns out to be spot on in terms of timing and stage presence. This is why the festival has grown at such a rapid pace – its organisers show huge commitment to the talent whilst also promoting the idea that it's a festival about the music and not simply about the dollar. It's a premise the audience gets behind too and their dedication and passion is part of what makes the festival such a success.

There are various reasons for its continued popularity, but many maintain it's down to who and what Andy Copping books each year. The co-founder and boss of the festival has stated that in the beginning their template was to be 'a rock version of Glastonbury with lots of different things going on but under the rock umbrella. Year on year that's been hard to achieve but I think we do it.' I think it's fair to say he absolutely smashes it!

Other rock/metal festivals such as Sonisphere have sprung up since its inception, but Download has the history that no other festival can compete with. Plus – and this is one of the best things about it – Download has its own mascot! The 'Download Dog', as he is affectionately known, is the only festival mascot in the country (unless you count the Worthy Farm cows!). The illustrated dog will vary from year to year but is a well-known and established part of the Download family. Over the years he has changed in appearance but that hasn't stopped hardcore fans having the beloved Download Dog tattooed on their bodies.

Download might sound like a festival that takes itself way too seriously but it's the complete opposite. Just one look at the on-site cinema sums up the mood of the festival perfectly: On the Friday they might show *Despicable Me 2*; on the Saturday they might choose *Anchorman 2* and the festival might close on the Sunday with *This Is Spinal Tap*. Something for the child and metal-head alike!

What's more, Download was one of the first festivals to embrace social networking, encouraging fans to have their say and to voice their thoughts and opinions. They really put the fans at the heart of the festival – encouraging their input and valuing their thoughts and ideas. Some fans are even invited to sit with Download organisers and discuss the festival face-to-face. Download's online interaction and forums are a key part of the success of the festival and something its organisers have won awards for. They took this kind of interaction to the next level during its first edition in 2003 when the festival tickets included a code that allowed festival goers to download tracks from bands on the bill.

Download currently has a licence for 120,000 people with five stages, but there are discussions taking place about adding further stages and entertainment pods for future years to offer the fans even more. And that also includes taking the Download brand global, just like its Monsters of Rock predecessor.

Like most other festivals there is a charitable element to their work and over the years Download has donated huge amounts of money to local charities and the surrounding community with both financial and educational support for local schools and colleges.

Aerosmith take the main stage by storm during the 2014 edition of Download.

Simon from Biffy Clyro, whose band first appeared at Download in 2005.

DOWNLOAD: THE FRIENDLIEST FESTIVAL EVER

It might surprise some people but time and time again bands, artists, fans and those who work at Download say that it is the friendliest festival they have ever been to. I totally agree: there is no ego or lofty expectations; in fact there is no other agenda for people except the music. Pretensions are left at the gate, along with aggression, rivalry and, indeed, any semblance of 'cool'. It might sound corny and unfamiliar but there is a feeling of family and belonging on-site, with a real emphasis on respect and acceptance of each other. When it comes to music, for me one of the most important elements of being a fan is having an open mind; at Download there's a real openness towards taste, opinion and choice – which is really refreshing compared to other more snobby genre festivals.

The population of Download comprises both newbies and a hardcore fan base, which has been maintained since the days of Monsters of Rock. In fact that's one of the greatest attributes of Download: it's a relatively young festival which has a great tradition and great history – and that is reflected in the type of people, both young and old, who attend the festival.

What's more it's a festival that doesn't have all the paraphernalia and unnecessary extra stuff going on. Its colour comes from the characters you see on site and on stage. Just by being there you feel like you are part of something special – a community or a collective. There is a kindred spirit of genuine excitement that pulsates throughout the audience

'THE POPULATION OF DOWNLOAD COMPRISES BOTH NEWBIES AND A HARDCORE FAN BASE, WHICH HAS BEEN MAINTAINED SINCE THE DAYS OF MONSTERS OF ROCK.'

and those performing, which thankfully means the festival doesn't surrender to chaos and piss throwing (unlike other, more infamous, genre festivals around the world).

THE MUSIC

Like any other self-respecting annual festival, it's all about the music at Download and there have been numerous highlights over the years: AC/DC played in 2010, a band who historically don't play festivals; Ramstein's performance in 2013 has been cited by many as the best headline performance ever at Download and topped off years of perseverance by the organisers to try and pin down the German metal band. Rage Against The Machine, Metallica and festival favourites Slipknot have also made appearances over the years. Indeed, Slipknot, who I must add are amazing, have appeared so many times over the years they have become honorary 'season ticket' holders – so much so there's a section on the festival website dedicated to 'Corey watch', referring to Corey Taylor, front man with Slipknot and Stone Sour, and how many times he has appeared at Download. It's currently running into double figures.

Linkin Park rock the main stage at Castle Donington.

A third stage, the Barfly Stage, was introduced in 2004, enhancing both the diversity and the size of the festival. It was a real showcase stage for those bands on the brink – the kinds of bands you were likely to see at Barfly venues. That name didn't last, of course (stage sponsorships never do), but it still has appeal for exciting bands. A fourth stage was welcomed in 2005 and at last count the festival was rocking out across five stages, yet again enhancing the diversity on show, catering for all tastes and pushing people's expectations.

What I like about the way that Download books bands is that they make no apologies for any decisions they make. There's always criticism, of course, and the aforementioned fans' forums didn't take the announcement of The Prodigy as 2012's headliners particularly well; the band itself more than proved its worth, though, and smashed the main stage on the Friday night. The Prodigy's appearance has opened the doors for bands such as Pendulum, Chase & Status and Biffy Clyro – a band who have the most impressive work ethic and determination of any band I know – to be taken seriously at Download. Biffy first appeared on the line-up back in 2005, pretty low down the bill on the main stage. Seven years later they soared to second from top, before headliners Metallica in 2012 – not bad going for three semi-naked blokes from Ayr!

It hasn't always been plain-sailing for the organisers at Download. The festival has had its fair share of cancellations over the years, as well as injuries, no shows and one band apparently (Saxon) turning up at the wrong Donington! To survive in the

'THERE IS A REASON THAT DOWNLOAD HAS BEEN VOTED TIME AND TIME AGAIN "BEST FESTIVAL" AT VARIOUS AWARDS CEREMONIES AND ANNUAL RETROSPECTIVES...'

industry it's important for a festival like Download to push the boundaries of what is expected of it. Rock fans have taken off their blinkers and seem happy to watch the festival branch out. The aforementioned feeling of community and shared experience also translates to the bands that play: there is almost a sense that they feel honoured to play there, as most of them used to go as a punter before being in a band.

Killswitch Engage perform at the 2014 edition of Download.

DOWNLOAD AND ME

I remember my first Download and feeling a sense of intimidation before I arrived on site. The feeling was something I had created in my own mind – I had formed preconceptions of how extreme it would be, even slightly menacing. How wrong could I be? Very. The festival is full of music fans and like-minded individuals with their own unique tastes but mutual respect.

There is a reason that Download has been voted time and time again 'best festival' at various awards ceremonies and annual retrospectives – and even in 2013 beating Glastonbury, Reading & Leeds and V Festival to be crowned Festival of the Year at the annual Festival Awards. I think it's because for this festival it is purely about the music, nothing else; it's also about a support network for bands, old and new, and for fans to see their favourite bands and artists, and to discover something that might surprise and even shock. Download has also learned from its predecessor's mistakes: having seen Monsters of Rock succumb to the natural cycles of music, there is now sensitivity towards taste, fashion and the culture of the contemporary music scene. As a result, Download is now one of the formative genre festivals and has the respect and loyalty from the music industry and punters alike.

Finally it is a real fans' festival. Download promotes a community that strives to be different, unique and to be proud of its beliefs. To be part of that kind of community, even for a day, is to be part of something quite special and memorable, and is something that everyone should strive to witness. When it comes to the music, what you are wearing, anything goes and no one bats an eyelid. Which is exactly as it should be.

Dirty Pretty Things drummer Gary Powell. An incredible drummer and a lovely man.

THE
ISLE
OF WIGHT
FESTIVAL

WHERE: *Seaclose Park*   **WHEN:** *Early June*

THE ISLE OF WIGHT FESTIVAL
Most likely to see:
A few bands on a ferry.

Scan here to see Edith's
Isle of Wight essentials.

The Doors, Jimi Hendrix, Janis Joplin, The Stones, The Who, Leonard Cohen, Joni Mitchell, Jethro Tull. Eight names that might not mean that much to today's pop-fuelled audience, but to the punters of the first Isle of Wight Festival back in 1968 they were *music*. Between its first and final edition in 1968 and 1970 respectively, the Isle of Wight single-handedly defined the festival experience: building upon the hippy-ethic of Woodstock, the Isle of Wight Festival brought something quintessentially British to the festival experience and in two short years became the blueprint for any music festival the world over. And today it remains perhaps one of the best festivals on the UK circuit.

THE EUROPEAN WOODSTOCK

The Isle of Wight Festival started in 1968 by the Foulk Brothers – Ron, Ray and Bill – and was seen as a 'hippy festival' with the ethos of peace, love and rock 'n' roll at its heart. Billed by some as the 'European Woodstock', around 15,000 people made their way to the island for its first edition, to watch the likes of Jefferson Airplane, Arthur Brown and Tyrannosaurus Rex. The following year saw Bob Dylan play his first live event since a near-fatal motorbike accident and the anticipation and excitement around his appearance alone was HUGE; this was supplemented, of course, with appearances from The Who and the legendary Bonzo Dog Doo-Dah Band – it was quite the line-up indeed!

Interest in the festival soared for its third edition, with a crowd of approximately 600,000 people descending on the Isle for another weekend of quality music and performance. The Who returned but this time the bill included the likes of Jimi Hendrix, Jethro Tull, Joni Mitchell, Leonard Cohen, Miles Davis, Emerson Lake & Palmer, Donovan and the mighty Doors. Just think – over half a million people congregating on one island to share the same musical experience. It's unbelievable! But it also resulted in the island being torn apart: with only 100,000 residents living on the normally peaceful and tranquil place, you can imagine the carnage after five times its population descended to listen to the biggest names in music.

The island has always had something quite magical and

Scan here to listen to Jake Bugg talk about his recent festival performances.

mystical about it, and considering it's only 23 miles wide and just over 13 miles long, for such a small place to have such a pull of musical gravity is pretty impressive. Some of its strange idiosyncrasies have gone down in music folklore: in 1970, for example, the south-westerly wind caused havoc with the sound system and Pink Floyd's PA was used to try and control the inconsistent sound levels. And yet it created an amazingly unique atmosphere,

'ISLE OF WIGHT, 1970: THE SOUNDS OF BOB DYLAN, JONI MITCHELL OR THE WHO CARRIED FROM THE SHORES OF THE COWES ESTUARY, ACROSS THE AFTON DOWN AND OUT INTO THE WILDERNESS OF THE ENGLISH CHANNEL.'

with the sounds of Bob Dylan, Joni Mitchell or The Who carried from the shores of the Cowes estuary, across the Afton Down and out into the wilderness of the English Channel.

If you ask me, those first few years on Wight sound like the archetypal festival experience. Thankfully there is so much fantastic old footage of performances and people arriving on site. I love watching films of the ferry trip – the

boats were like busker transporters, with each deck overflowing with amateur guitarists and tambourine players, most of whom probably had no idea what they were about to witness. John Giddings, a music agent and promoter who has worked with the likes of The Rolling Stones, Madonna, Iggy Pop and David Bowie, attended the festival in 1970. At the time he was only 16 years old but it made a lasting impression on him, so much so that it's down to him that the festival got a second wind. Giddings describes that first impression as 'Gorilla Warfare; it was like a religious pilgrimage with the most extraordinary bonding between these people who liked the same music as me, I had no idea. It really gave me a meaning to life.' John remembers that when Jimi Hendrix played you were able to walk all the way down to the front, weaving your way through the seated crowd and get to the barrier. I wonder when and why that changed.

The original Isle of Wight Festival was always doomed to have a short shelf life. A vociferous opposition to the festival naturally grew from the local residents – with many understandably disapproving of the large influx of music lovers descending on their island and causing havoc to the infrastructure. In fact the legendary festival made an indelible stamp on festival folklore in more ways than one.

THE ISLE OF WIGHT TODAY

After some half a million music lovers descended on the island for the 1970 edition, the government introduced The Isle of Wight Act, which prevented a crowd of more than 5,000 gathering together in one place on one night. This meant that anyone organising a festival had to gain permission not only from the landowner (obviously!) but also for a licence from the local council. Anything from the tiniest get together to a fully-fledged music extravaganza required permission from numerous authorities and the bureaucracy of the process significantly affected the amount of festivals popping up across the UK. It was quite a legacy – and one the Isle of Wight organisers took a long time to live down.

Indeed, it wasn't until some 32 years after its last event that the residents of the Isle of Wight relented and allowed a new and improved festival to take place on the sandy shores of the UK's largest island. In fact the Isle of Wight council were desperate to get the festival up and running again and approached pretty much everyone in the music business. No one was interested, however, because despite the overwhelming success of its late 1960s incarnation, the idea of having a festival that you could only get to by ferry seemed like a preposterous idea.

The aforementioned John Giddings got behind it and helped the council get it off the ground. The festival promoter used his personal experience and affinity for the original festival to create a family-friendly reboot where all kinds of people could come together and watch their favourite bands and join in one big party. In fact it was John's idea that people take life seriously for 51 weeks of the year but should allow themselves a week to come down and do what they want to do, with no one pushing them around. So in 2002 the festival got its second chance on a different site and under the name 'Rock Island'; it was only on for one day and welcomed a crowd of about 10,000. The festival resurrected its original moniker 12 months later and the first Isle of Wight Festival

'IT'S NOT JUST ABOUT KEEPING THE BANDS AND ARTISTS HAPPY, IT'S ABOUT MAKING SURE THE AUDIENCE IS HAVING A GOOD TIME TOO.'

Flea entertains the crowd as Red Hot Chili Peppers headline the Isle of Wight in 2014.

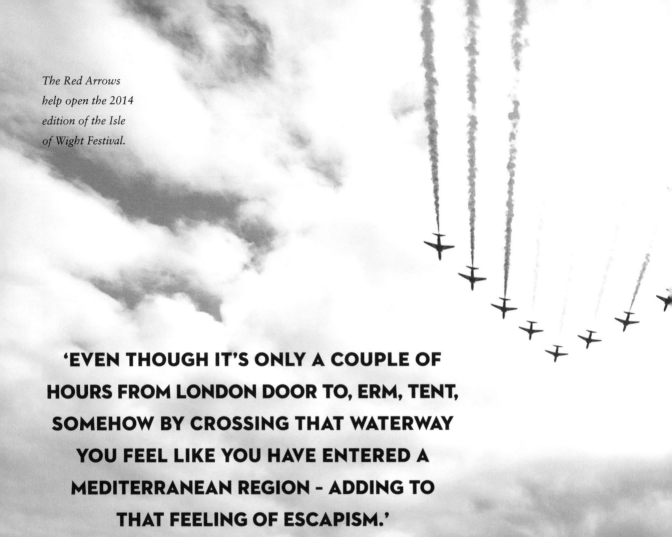

'EVEN THOUGH IT'S ONLY A COUPLE OF HOURS FROM LONDON DOOR TO, ERM, TENT, SOMEHOW BY CROSSING THAT WATERWAY YOU FEEL LIKE YOU HAVE ENTERED A MEDITERRANEAN REGION – ADDING TO THAT FEELING OF ESCAPISM.'

of the 21st century welcomed some 50,000 people to see the likes of Paul Weller and Bryan Adams rock its newly built main stage.

The festival today isn't a huge commercial beast run to make loads of money; in fact the money they do make gets pumped back into making it more fun for the people concerned. John Giddings, for instance, lost £500,000 in the first year of running the festival in 2003, but as he says, 'it's called investment in the future'. The organisers obsess all year round to think of more ways to encourage the crowd to enjoy themselves; it's not just about keeping the bands and artists happy for them, it's about making sure the audience is having a good time. For example, when the Rolling Stones were due to play in 2007 they told the organisers

they weren't bringing their B-stage, which normally took Mick et al right into the heart of the audience. Nevertheless, the organisers forked out an extra £100,000 to have the stage in place for just three songs to be played in the middle of the park. The festival also pumps money into local charities and island-based organisations, especially for young people where music plays a positive role in their lives. 'Do the Wight Thing' is a festival initiative that supports local charities, including St Catherine's which raises funds and awareness for children and young people with speech, language and communication needs.

The site is an easy one to navigate (it's on an island, after all!). It's pretty compact with the biggest focal point being the main stage which stands at the head of the main

arena. Year on year there are always slight changes to the smaller tents and areas, whether that be a sponsor change a movement of location or additions. There are also areas tailored to tie in with things going on in the world outside the festival that the audience will still want to be part of; the Field of Dreams area, for example, showed the World Cup in 2014 and also showed films for anyone who wanted to take a breather from the music. Walking away from the main stage you pass the acoustic stage and head towards Strawberry Fields and the Big Top – a second stage which always has a fantastic and varied line-up, but also acts as the dance stage, so you might also catch Groove Armada or DJ Fresh playing there, or even Primal Scream, The Vaccines, or Tom Jones. Next to that you have the Silent Arena, which isn't actually silent as that would defeat the purpose of a festival, but includes 'silent discos' and other such delights. The Strawberry Fields isn't the only Beatles-themed area, there's also an 'Octopus's Garden', and on the way back to your tent you might walk down 'Penny Lane', out towards the back of the festival, which is a nice touch. You might also pass the Hard Rock Rising Stage and various other branded tents and areas. The Kids' Zone is well-stocked with things for the kids to do, including the Rainbow Stage, which offers storytelling, magicians doing their thing and a variety of musicians.

One of the things I noticed about the Isle of Wight is the microclimate it enjoys. Even though it's only a couple of hours from London, door to, erm, tent, somehow by crossing that waterway you feel like you have entered a Mediterranean region – adding to that feeling of escapism.

THE PEOPLE

I can't really say there is a particular type of person that goes to the Isle of Wight Festival; it appeals to a wide range of age groups and musical allegiances. The festival has a real family vibe and caters for a wide range of demographics and ages. The local islanders make up a large percentage of the attendees, many of whom choose to take full advantage of such an amazing festival on their doorstep. I guess for them there is also a sense of pride, not just by having the festival there every year, but the heritage of this event; it's known worldwide, it's revered and draws some of the world's biggest and best artists. True music fans attend the Isle of Wight, and for some, attending the festival is almost a rite of passage – not just for young

Right: Paul Smith from Maximo Park plays to the crowd. I love the way you can hear his accent when he sings – something a lot of people shy away from.

'THE ISLE OF WIGHT IS KNOWN WORLDWIDE, IT'S REVERED AND DRAWS SOME OF THE WORLD'S BIGGEST AND BEST ARTISTS.'

people but also for a real mixture of generations. That is one of the many things that John Giddings remembers about his experience of that early incarnation of the Isle of Wight: 'the experience bonds people – you can sit and talk to strangers because you are having a shared experience.' I like that and for me it's a big part of being at any festival – it's your festival, hope to make new friends, catch someone's eye and smile as you share in the experience of watching a truly exciting band.

THE MUSIC OF THE ISLE OF WIGHT

One of the most enduring aspects of the Isle of Wight Festival is the music. As previously mentioned, the original editions of the festival were at the forefront of contemporary music; the organisers cherry-picked some of the greatest and most zeitgeist performers to entertain its hordes of music fans.

Perhaps the festival's most famous performer was Jimi Hendrix. The short-lived guitar magician played the 1970 edition of the festival and his performance has endured long in the memory of many subsequent performers to play the main stage. Jay-Z, Foo Fighters and Sir Paul McCartney have all honoured the legendary musician in their own way – the last of whom churned out a few bars of Hendrix's 'Purple Haze' before launching into his final song in 2010.

Talking of legends of the festival, The Doors' Jim Morrison spoke incredibly coherently the day after he played the festival in 1970, praising the organisation of such a large music event. He also went on to explain how there was definitely a huge romanticism around Woodstock and what the festival managed to achieve, which was due partly to the film that had been made about the legendary festival. What should have been a celebration of young culture turned into something else, and he hoped that people would return to cities under the Woodstock spell. This romanticism eventually spread across the Atlantic, before hitting the southern shores of the UK and manifesting itself as the Isle of Wight Festival. Indeed Morrison took playing at festivals seriously, and would regularly find time to get out and wander around the campsites and enjoy getting the chance to talk to people and get a real sense of the festival.

The Isle of Wight Festival has

Above: Rudimental rock the main stage in 2014.

played host to so many different acts since its rebirth in 2002: David Bowie, Muse, The Strokes, Neil Young, Bruce Springsteen, Pearl Jam, Calvin Harris, Faithless, and REM. The Who made a return in 2004 and I can't think of many bands that have such a long-standing relationship with any festival, particularly since their last appearance was 34 years ago!

Today more than 60 bands and artists from a wide spectrum of the music industry play across a number of stages. Of all the bands that John Giddings wants to attract to play the festival, he always seems to come back to Blur and Oasis. He would love to see Blur headline the main stage on a Saturday night, and Oasis, well who knows, maybe when they reform!

Fleetwood Mac were also on his wish list and after years of trying John finally confirmed them as the headliners for the 2015 edition. Of their return to the festival circuit, the band said, 'we've always wanted to come to the UK to play The Isle of Wight Festival, and so we are delighted that in 2015 we are finally making it happen! So many of our fellow artists and friends have played at this historic event over the years, and we can't wait to see all of our fans on the island next summer.' What a coup for the festival – they're a band that everyone has been trying to secure and their billing is a testament to the festival's reputation and the clout that Giddings has with artists old and new.

THE ISLE OF WIGHT FESTIVAL AND ME

There were a good few years when Isle of Wight was a bit of a ritual outing for me. In fact the strange pop-up backstage bar/accommodation in the form of a travel lodge has witnessed some extraordinary karaoke sessions from me and various others over the years. My very dear friends Vicky and Gemma both share the same birthday around the same dates as the Isle of Wight Festival and it was always a good excuse to celebrate with one of our favourite pastimes. Vicky used to work for Coldplay and in 2006, the year they headlined, we watched from picnic tables at the front of the stage as Chris encouraged the enormous crowd to sing 'Happy Birthday' to her. Lou Reed also headlined the same year, although he didn't really get into the festival spirit by playing an hour of unrecognisable tunes with not a hit in sight. That was until Coldplay came on and provided some welcome relief by playing 'Perfect Day'!

Sometimes with artists you have to see them live to fully understand and to fully click with them. I had that with Pink at Isle of Wight in 2010. Although I'd played her music on the radio for years I'd never really been to one of her shows; but when I saw she was playing at Isle of Wight, I wanted to see what she was like live. Her arrival basically involved her jumping from a box attached to a crane about 100 feet above the crowd in front of the main stage; then she completely nailed her vocal even whilst being flown over the audience on a pretty impressive harness, or zorbing over the crowd during her guitarist's rather over-the-top guitar solo. The woman has skills and a very impressive set of lungs on her, and all those other female pop stars of recent years who never attempt to sing live should take a leaf out of Pink's book. It was a memorable and accomplished performance.

> 'THE ISLE OF WIGHT FESTIVAL IS ABOUT PROVIDING GOOD MUSICAL ENTERTAINMENT FOR PEOPLE OF DIFFERENT AGES WITH MUSIC FROM THE PAST, THE PRESENT AND THE FUTURE.'

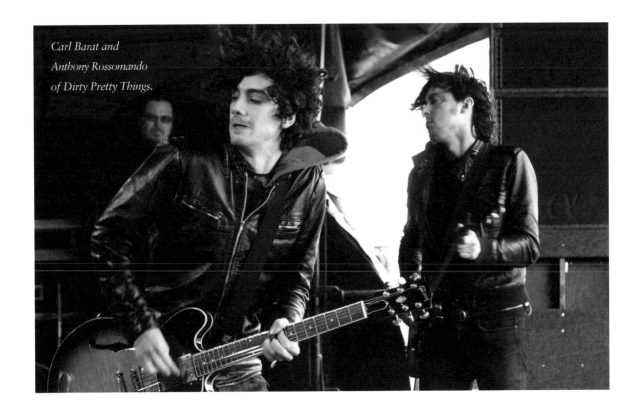

Carl Barat and Anthony Rossomando of Dirty Pretty Things.

A FESTIVAL FOR MUSIC LOVERS

I love the simplicity of the Isle of Wight Festival. It's about providing good musical entertainment for people of different ages with music from the past, the present and the future. That, of course, may seem like the aim of most festivals, but not all of them achieve it!

I'm going to leave you with something that Jim Morrison said back in 1970 when he was asked about the future of festivals: 'I've never played anything like this before, we didn't think our music was styled or would hold up in huge outdoor events but we were wrong. And all those people who say that huge festivals are over – that they are dead – well I think they are wrong, they are going to become even more significant over the next three to five years.' If only he was around now to see how far we have come: real music has been this festival's heritage; it is something the organisers constantly refer back to, to drive the festival towards the future. It's a festival for real music lovers of all ages.

WHERE: *Somerset*   **WHEN:** *Last weekend of June*

GLASTONBURY *Most likely to see*: A naked granny in Jesus sandals, walking through the Green Fields without a care in the world (I actually saw one back in 2004!).

SCAN HERE

Scan here to see Edith's Glastonbury essentials.

Nothing can really prepare you for the experience of Glastonbury. It's so much more than a music festival; it is an epic celebration of contemporary music and performing arts, and its history is enshrouded in the counter-cultural and free-festival movements from which it sprouted back in 1970. Back then the 'Pilton Pop, Blues and Folk Festival', as it was originally known, had only 1,500 attendees, cost £1 and with that you got a free carton of milk! Nowadays, the mere mention of a music festival – anywhere in the world – and Glastonbury will be the first that pings into the brain, whether you have been lucky enough to go or not.

'THE 1971 EDITION FEATURED THE LIKES OF DAVID BOWIE, FAIRPORT CONVENTION AND JOAN BAEZ, ALL OF WHOM CAME TOGETHER IN SUPPORT OF ITS "FREE-FESTIVAL" IDEAL.'

THE HISTORY OF GLASTO

'The Best Festival in the World' is a phrase that is often thrown around by artists who play, and music and art lovers who attend Glastonbury – and for very good reason too. Michael Eavis, West-Country farmer and founder of the festival, has always had a passion for music, the arts and creativity, and his personal love and affection is at the heart of the festival and what it stands for. When he was registering the 'Glastonbury' company, Eavis wrote: 'The Glastonbury Festival aims to encourage and stimulate youth culture from around the world in all its forms, including pop music, dance music, jazz, folk music, fringe theatre, drama, mime, circus, cinema, poetry and all the creative forms.' Glastonbury Festival provides a platform for each of these forms in its own unique way: it is a festival, a celebration, a commitment and a community, and if you put the effort in you will reap the benefits.

Glastonbury in its current guise is rather different to its original one back in 1970. The 1971 edition featured the likes of David Bowie, Fairport Convention and Joan Baez, all of whom came together in support of its 'free-festival' ideal – a feast of music and performing arts, all provided free of charge. This particular spirit has been rather diluted over the years and was brought into focus by the 'commercialised' editions, which

One of my favourite artists ever! Karen O performs with Yeah Yeah Yeahs on the Other Stage at Glastonbury in 2009. I walked past the band after the show and went complete 'fan girl' on her.

began to take hold at the end of the 20th century. But Glastonbury has always been a 'moveable feast': from the early 'free spirited' years of the late 1970s when hippies would flock to the festival in droves (by the festival's second year the attendance had increased to a massive 12,000 people!), through to the rough and ready years of the 1980s and 1990s when policing, rioting and ticketing issues forced the festival to go through a period of reinvention, Glastonbury has always been at the forefront of the festival experience throughout the world.

It hasn't, of course, always been plain sailing for festival founder and chief visionary Michael Eavis. The sad passing of his wife Jean, in 1999, changed so many things. The two of them had planned to retire in 2000 and bid farewell to an institution they

co-founded some 30 years previous. At the time the festival was entering a difficult period and the Eavises were convinced it had run its course. Yet after Jean's passing Michael realised he needed the festival more than ever, and with the dedication and support of his daughter Emily, the festival was reinvented. Its new guise became a touching tribute to Jean and all the work and love she put into the festival. For Emily – the festival's organiser from 2000 – the project was never meant to be a long term one, although she has since found herself living on the farm with her husband and kids. She's grown into quite the curator and books the bands for the Pyramid and Parks stages, as well as managing the festival's growing sponsorship.

Indeed the work has been so intense and the festival so demanding

*Chris Martin
having fun.*

that occasionally the organisers have had a few years off. The break in 1991 was to allow organisers to 'rethink the festival', while five years later, in 1996, the festival had its first 'rest' year to allow the land to recover from the endless welly boots and general wear and tear of the Worthy Farm fields. This became a pattern thereafter, with a 'gap' year occurring once every five years – although the organisers opted for a 'gap' in 2012 due to the London Olympic Games and the apparent lack of Portaloos across the southern part of England! The next 'rest' year has been confirmed for 2017.

Every year has its own unique legend – whether that's due to the legendary headliners or the legendary weather. Glastonbury has not been without its problems – there have been issues with local councils, protestors, security, technology, and even the controversial 'security fence' – but its biggest adversary has always been the Great British weather. The highest rainfall in 45 years was recorded in 1982, with five inches of rain falling on the Friday night. In 1983 organisers were forced to start applying for a licence for the festival after changes in the law, facing a whole new era of disruption, and in 1986, 1987 and 1989 they were refused a licence but won after taking the case to court. But the rain isn't necessarily the only problem: add a low-lying dairy farm and some 100,000 excitable punters and you will find tons of slippery and rather annoying mud baths, which slowly but surely turn into sticky, knee-high 'death-walks'.

THE FESTIVAL TODAY: ITS STAGES, MAGIC, MUSIC AND POLITICS

When you're at Glastonbury you'll find the majority of these 'death-walks' only lead one way: towards the Pyramid Stage – the jewel in the festival's hippie crown. Enchanting, majestic and completely unique, the Pyramid Stage is known the world over as *the* platform for any aspiring musician: once you're on that stage and performing in front of nearly 100,000 music aficionados then you know you've made it. Originally built for the 1971 edition and based on the Great Pyramid of Giza in

Egypt, the iconic stage burnt down in 1994 only a few days before the festival began, and was rebuilt in full at the start of the new millennium.

The Pyramid Stage began life in a dream. Stage designer Bill Harkin, on the eve of the second edition of the festival in 1971, dreamt of two beams of light connecting behind the head of a festival goer. After conducting research into lay lines and consulting a number of druids and fellow festival goers, the base of the original site in the Vale Of Avalon was formed – itself being 100th part of the base area of the Great Pyramid of Giza in Egypt. A rather ambitious construction, the project was partly funded by a weekly event held at The Roundhouse in Camden called 'Implosion', run by DJ Jeff Dexter and Ian Knight, who was also a pioneering stage and lighting director. Kwickform was used for the frame and towers – a system used in shipbuilding and a method of construction, which up until then had never been used outside a dry dock. Today it is the staging industries' system of choice the world over. Once the stage had been erected, the matter of cladding was extended to festival goers, who were unaware of the intricate nature of the metal sheets they were attaching. Finally, over five million light-reflecting facets were added, a design feature that turned the Pyramid Stage into the most iconic and beautiful structure in all music festival history. But, in keeping with the environmental ideals of the festival, it only required two 10kw lights to turn the whole stage into what looked like a giant 'wonderful shining diamond.'

New stages and areas have cropped up over the years, owing to the never-ending growth of the festival. The first Classical Music tent was erected in 1980; fifteen years later the Dance Tent appeared, with Massive Attack headlining a memorable debut set. The latter was transformed into the dance village in 2005 and is the place to go when the Pyramid and 'Other' Stage close at around 11pm. The Glade area was opened in 2000 after Michael witnessed an impromptu rave in the 1990s. It's a fantastic area of musical discovery, which returned to its home amongst the trees in the summer of 2014, and has since grown into a natural home for experimentalism and beats. It sits between the Avalon Field and the site of the Dance Tent, 'housing' the likes of Orbital, The Orb, Stanton Warriors and Jon Hopkins, to name but a small few.

The New Talent tent became the John Peel Stage in 2005, following the legendary DJ's untimely death, and in 2007 Emily Eavis introduced

'THE PYRAMID STAGE BEGAN LIFE IN A DREAM...'

The Park Stage, a staggeringly valuable and influential platform for musicians. To be part of the line-up on this stage is seen as not only an honour for established bands, it's also an opportunity for those artists on the brink of something huge to progress to the next level. There's also a large selection of 'minor' stages, which you can find as you delve deeper and further away from the beaten path.

This is key to the Glasto-magic: it is enormous. The festival is situated within 900 acres of the Vale of Avalon – an area rich in mythology, religious folklore and symbolism. Over the years the festival has grown rapidly, not just in numbers but also over the land mass it covers, making it the seventh largest (albeit temporary!) 'city' in the south of England. At its busiest the pop-up 'metropolis' houses over 200,000 people within its intricate infrastructure – an infrastructure that is a huge undertaking, and that takes an incredible amount of planning and organisation: from the campsites, stages, car parks, toilets, walk-in medical centre, property lock-up, welfare area and travel centre, to the campsite stewards, security, engineers, technicians, and even CCTV (ironically most of which we don't see but most definitely take for granted and don't give a second thought).

Another area where Glastonbury has had a very strong voice about is politics and social issues. The festival has always been ahead of the game when it comes to important issues that affect people and the planet, and it seems the rest of the world is normally playing catch-up with what Glastonbury stands for on a social platform, whether that be the

Below:
Willie Nelson
performs at
Glastonbury.

disarmament of nuclear weapons or environmental issues. A huge amount of money has been donated to worthy causes over the years, including Oxfam, Campaign for Nuclear Disarmament, Greenpeace, and Water Aid. Further beneficiaries are worldwide children's charities, which assist special schools throughout the Somerset and Avon region.

NAVIGATING GLASTO... (AND FINDING THOSE SECRET GIGS!)

Some festivals have two elements to the site: one where the performances happen and one where you are supposed to sleep. With Glastonbury there is no separation, nothing really closes down, the main stages stop after the headliners but there is life after headliners. Of course there are campsites and quite a lot of them, but the site never shuts down – you are free to roam the lands from dusk till dawn! That, for me is what makes the festival magical, and it is where you can find unexpected pleasures – the extraordinary sights and sounds that are a far cry from what is on the main line-up. Whispers of secret sets and collaborations start from whenever you set foot on site; some are complete fabrication, of course, but when they do turn out to be true you might discover Thom Yorke DJ-ing with Nigel Godrich in the back of a tiny pop-up bar! Those are the moments that make the experience unique, amongst the rolling hills of Somerset: the sight of the sunrise sat up on a hill with the Stone Circle in the foreground is a pretty special and spiritual moment, even for the most prolific atheist.

The festival's size and variety thus means it is a commitment on a number of levels. To fully embrace

'WHISPERS OF SECRET SETS AND COLLABORATIONS START FROM WHENEVER YOU SET FOOT ON SITE; SOME ARE COMPLETE FABRICATION, OF COURSE, BUT WHEN THEY DO TURN OUT TO BE TRUE YOU MIGHT DISCOVER THOM YORKE DJ-ING WITH NIGEL GODRICH IN THE BACK OF A TINY POP-UP BAR!'

Left: Foals' Yannis sits in the sunshine backstage at Glastonbury. Foals, for me, have become one of the festival's greats.

You always get an amazing view from the top of the Glastonbury hill.

'THERE IS AN EXTRAORDINARY, WEIRD, INEXPLICABLE MAGNETISM IN THE EARTH AND THAT'S WHY IT'S SPECIAL. WHEN THOSE POINTS OF TRUE COMMUNE BETWEEN THE MUSIC AND THE PEOPLE HAPPEN, IT'S LIKE NOTHING ELSE. IT'S A BIT LIKE THE HOLY GRAIL OF FESTIVALS, IF YOU GET IT RIGHT.' – DAMON ALBARN ON GLASTO

the festival and realise the potential on offer you should stay on site and aim to be there for the whole duration, not just the Friday – Sunday 'high season'. Some 'devotees' even spend their annual summer holiday on Worthy Farm – in fact a friend of mine once spent a full eight days on site, although that might be taking it a little too far! The site is open from the Monday before the main weekend begins and you can arrive whenever you like. There is a reason that people get there early, and that might be the difference between a half hour walk and half a day's walk (slight exaggeration!) back to your tent from the far-flung corners of the festival. You want a good spot for camping and a good spot for getting off site on the Monday morning; it would also be good to have a good spot close to the main areas, in case you happened to leave an important item that you can't live without.

Over the years I've experienced a variety of sleeping arrangements – and I use the term 'sleeping' loosely: from falling into the boot of my car; sharing a minuscule tin can-sized caravan behind the Pyramid Stage with my TV partner in crime at the time Colin Murray (never again); waking up in a tent with half a metre of water operating as a moat around my sleeping bag thanks to my friends, who very kindly agreed to put our tent up but forgot to put on the important small top vent

sheet; or staying 20 minutes from site above a pub and bussing back and forth – I've pretty much done them all. Each one provided a lifetime of memories and enjoyment, as well as providing the appropriate amount of lodging for what I was doing that particular year. Glastonbury is the festival I have been to the most, the festival I've spent most time at, the festival that I've made the biggest commitment to, so forgive me if I slip into the odd nostalgic dalliance. As mentioned in the Introduction to this guide, it was the place I visited two weeks after having a c-section to present the BBC coverage, which meant regular visits to the production Portakabin, which became my makeshift nursing room. I missed it by a few weeks, but keep in mind if you happen to give birth at the festival then you can look forward to a lifelong free entry!

Indeed, Glastonbury can be what you want it to be – it can be customised to cater for all tastes. Whether you are going with mates or as a family with kids, there's something for everyone. No one is going to be bored – quite the opposite! I've done it in a number of guises, both as a punter and while working for the BBC. Working at the festival restricts how much you can see and do, but I don't tend to let that stop me, particularly if I'm residing in the aforementioned caravan behind the Pyramid Stage.

My fun begins at midnight when work is finished and I can search out those exemplary dark corners of the site and stay up till dawn. It's the best time to go exploring and you see some incredible sights. The first year I arrived on the Friday night as Coldplay took to the main stage and met up with friends who had been before; that was a great help as they knew the site and it was a good opportunity to get a sense of scale, location and points of interest.

THE MUSIC

I haven't really touched on the music at Glastonbury in any great detail and that is genuinely because there is so much other stuff going on! Everyone's experience of music at Glastonbury is very unique to the individual, and even if you come as a group you might never see any of the same bands as your mates for the entire weekend. In fact you could possibly spend the entire weekend listening and watching artists you've never heard before – which is quite a rarity these days! Pretty much everyone who can and wants to play it has played it and, just like the spirit of its first edition in 1970, if they pull out then another band will offer to step in and fill the slot.

It would be impossible to try and give an overview of the bands and artists that have played Glastonbury over the past 40 years. Rumours for the festival's headliners normally begin a few months into the New Year once all the tickets have sold out, but needless to say Glastonbury is definitely one of those festivals where you can tick off heritage artists that might be on your wish list: the likes of Sir Paul McCartney, Stevie Wonder, Rolling Stones, Neil Young, Dolly Parton, Brian Wilson, Shirley Bassey, The Who and Leonard Cohen have all made appearances at the UK's largest festival. There are the unconfirmed 'secret shows' too: over the course of the weekend you'll see droves of punters rushing to certain areas of the site in the hope of seeing a 'rumoured' band or DJ show up for an unbilled set. Radiohead, Pulp and Skrillex have made 'secret' appearances in recent years.

Don't make plans, the best laid ones never occur at Glastonbury. Understand this – you haven't paid the money to watch your favourite band – you've paid for the experience and you will discover arts you never knew you were into, genres of music you never knew existed and you will be a part of 'the best festival in the world'.

Right:
Snoop entertains
the Pyramid Stage.
I would hate to have
to guess how much
his knuckle-duster
mic holder is worth!

'DON'T MAKE PLANS,
THE BEST-LAID ONES
NEVER OCCUR AT
GLASTONBURY.'

LONDON FESTIVALS

Most likely to see: A traffic warden with a smile
and having a little boogie.

Scan here to see Edith's
London festivals essentials.

Many cities have a vibrant cultural calendar that is chock-full of effervescent and eye-catching music events. From the local acoustic club to the municipal park performances, cities are blessed with some of the most exciting live music events of the year. More recently, however, city festivals have become almost a sub-culture amongst the festival circuit, with metropolises such as London, Manchester and Brighton all introducing citywide festivals at some point during the year.

The first city-based festival I attended, however, was on the continent – Primavera in Barcelona, back in 2004. At the time it was located in the grounds of the outdoor architectural museum Poble Espanyol, close to the 1992 Olympic Stadium and at the foot of the mountain of Monujuïc. I had never seen anything like Primavera: it was colourful, vibrant, busy and exciting, and its urban landscape served as a refreshing counterpoint to the muddy pits and rolling fields of the UK festival scene. The location at Poble Espanyol really was very unique and it's a shame Primavera moved in 2005 to its current location

at Parc del Forum. The experience of climbing the twisted cobbled streets and coming across pockets of music (whilst dodging the pick-pockets!) and not really understanding how you got there or where you go next, was enchanting. In fact the whole experience was pretty magical and extraordinary considering it's just a few miles from the city centre of Barcelona – a city that never sleeps at the best of times and has a life-long heritage with cultural and musical explosions.

London also has a fantastic history and reputation with music – particularly live music – if only they would stop building train lines through some of the most legendary venues in the city (I miss the Astoria dearly!). Whether you attend the Notting Hill Carnival, Camden Crawl or just hang out in and around the Southbank area, London really entices you to investigate all manner of cultural offerings. Indeed, the Southbank area is a fertile ground for an assortment of creative stimulation, let alone music. I have been lucky enough to watch numerous bands perform within the beauty of the

'WHETHER YOU ATTEND THE NOTTING HILL CARNIVAL, CAMDEN CRAWL OR JUST HANG OUT IN AND AROUND THE SOUTHBANK AREA, LONDON REALLY ENTICES YOU TO INVESTIGATE ALL MANNER OF CULTURAL OFFERINGS.'

Star Wars-esque Royal Festival Hall – including The National, Badly Drawn Boy, Calexico and the Royal Philharmonic Orchestra. It's a bit like watching a gig in a museum!

The Hall also hosts a number of events for the annual Meltdown Festival, again proving itself as the premier venue for music, art, performance and film in London. Meltdown, as the title might indicate, breaks down the musical influences and experiences of a certain high-profile curator and celebrates them in the form of various events over a number of days. The festival began back in 1993 with conductor George Benjamin appointed guest director for the inaugural year, and each subsequent year a curator is appointed who invites various artists to perform, talk, divulge and exhibit their work. Over the years curators have included Nick Cave, Patti Smith, Yoko Ono and in 2014, James Lavelle.

There are plenty of other spots, locations and venues around London that regularly draw out not just creativity but also crowds in abundance. London is creatively inspiring, it's renowned the world over for its culture, its history and most certainly its music. From opera houses to theatres, legendary music venues to galleries, the city is awash with opportunities to watch, listen and be inspired. Outside space is also something that, for a capital city, London has plenty of: Hyde Park, Regent's Park, Kew Gardens, Richmond Park, the Olympic Park to name but a few. Victoria Park in east London has become a regular site for a number of London's live music events and festivals, and following a £12million refurbishment, has recently seen its old features restored and repaired, and live music facilities brought bang up to date. In fact Victoria was the first public park in London to be built specifically for the people (it opened in 1843), so it seems apt that people's favourite Lovebox and Field Day have used it as a site over the years.

I could have written an entire book on London and all it has to offer musically but what I wanted to do was give you an idea of the variety of events the city has to offer, just a few of the best and most fun. Here are a few of the best London festivals around…

LOVEBOX,
VICTORIA PARK,
JULY

Lovebox was originally held in Clapham Common but now takes place in Victoria Park in London in mid-July. You might recognise the name from Groove Armada's fourth album: Andy Cato and Tom Findlay, aka Groove Armada, founded the festival in the same year the album was released in 2002 as a kind of extravagant album launch party. Now over ten years old, Lovebox attracts 75,000 people over the weekend and is considered one of London's premier city festivals.

Tom and Andy wanted the line-up for the festival to encapsulate the multicultural nature of the capital, combining 'legendary with the future'. Yes, it's a music

festival; yes, it's a dance festival; yes, it's a day festival if you want it to be; and yes, you might see Duran Duran, Sly and the Family Stone, Snoop Dog, Brian Ferry or Katy B, Rudimental, Jurassic 5 as well as Annie Mac at some point during the weekend! One should think of Lovebox as a drive through someone's eclectic music collection – someone who you've assumed always was a dance head! There is a real carnival spirit about the festival; you might hear some ska, some soul classics or even a bit of hip hop for good measure; it has a real party atmosphere. There is also an authenticity to the festival and that comes from the attention to detail with

'NOW OVER TEN YEARS OLD, LOVEBOX ATTRACTS 75,000 PEOPLE OVER THE WEEKEND AND IS CONSIDERED ONE OF LONDON'S PREMIER CITY FESTIVALS.'

Scan here to find out how the thriving live music scene shaped Paul McCartney's festival experience.

'THERE IS ALSO AN AUTHENTICITY TO THE FESTIVAL AND THAT COMES FROM THE ATTENTION TO DETAIL WITH THE LINE-UP, AS WELL AS THE FAMILIAR AND CHARACTERFUL LOCATION IN THE HEART OF EAST LONDON.'

the line-up, as well as the familiar and characterful location in the heart of east London.

One thing that Lovebox really excels at far beyond any of its counterparts is its emphasis on being child-friendly; in fact many parental music fans who live in and around London use it as pseudo-indoctrination into festival culture for their kids. An adult must accompany you if you are under 16 and there's a cap of four under-16s per adult. Tickets are free if you are under 12 but you still have to have a ticket to gain entry. Things start at the usual time even in city festivals, so bands can be kicking off at midday and it's well worth getting yourself (and your kids!) up, out and ready to party early-doors.

Lovebox, just like its country-based counterparts, relies heavily on the weather to be a success, but with one important caveat: its accessibility. If you live 20 minutes away, it's pouring it down and your day ticket has cost you less than £50, you might, sinfully, decide to do the DIY that's been staring you in the face for months instead. You have a greater choice to not go, where as if you have made the effort to travel halfway across the country to a festival that costs you half a month's mortgage, you will automatically put in more effort! Thus, if the sun is out, it's going to be busier and, of course, a lot more lively; but that's the harsh reality of our Great British summers – a sunny day really is priceless!

It is also in London: you're in a gorgeous park, surrounded by tents and stages, and the world of a festival manifests itself. It really is quite a sight! But you are never far from a reminder of just how close you are to the centre of a city – Tower Hamlets high-rises speck the skyline and the urban architecture itself becomes part of the atmosphere of the festival. I love it and it makes the festival even more commoving.

Right: Lily entertains the crowd.

WIRELESS FESTIVAL –
FINSBURY PARK, JULY

The Wireless Festival has been on the go since 2005 in various large sites across London: between 2005 and 2012 it was held in Hyde Park, before being moved to the Olympic Park in Stratford in 2013. The 2014 edition saw the festival moved to Finsbury Park for the first time – with headliners Kanye West and Bruno Mars providing the irresistible soundtrack for a blissed-out summer night in London town.

Organised by Live Nation, Wireless is a commercial juggernaut, which secures some of the biggest music acts around the world – predominantly 'names' with huge marketability. Over the years the festival has branched out to add shows in Birmingham and Leeds. It normally takes place over the first weekend in July and tends to favour the dance and R'n'B genres as opposed to when it first began with acts such as The Strokes, The White Stripes, Keane and Kasabian headlining.

Indeed, Wireless is about mass appeal and draws in huge crowds to watch acts on the three or four stages. And just like Lovebox, it's a weekend-long festival in a city, but with no camping. The framework for a park festival is always the same, just the name and sponsor change. I remember when I was on Capital Radio many moons ago, hosting a radio show with my very dear friend Cat Deeley. We were part of The Prince's Trust 'Party In The Park', a huge pop party put on by the radio station to raise money for the Prince of Wales' charity. The party was fairly similar to that of Wireless, and while it has now moved to Finsbury Park, nothing has changed in its appeal or its vibe.

I like to try to get out of London to watch gigs as often as possible, mainly because sometimes I get the feeling London crowds can be spoilt for choice. It's funny to hear people in bands talk about London crowds – many of them repeating the notion that they are never an easy crowd to please, you really have to put the work in to earn their support and love. But when you get them onside and they reciprocate that effort, there can be no feeling like it in the world – particularly at a live event as large as Wireless.

Everytime I've been to an event in Hyde Park the main issue for me has been the noise restriction. I want to *feel* the music at a live

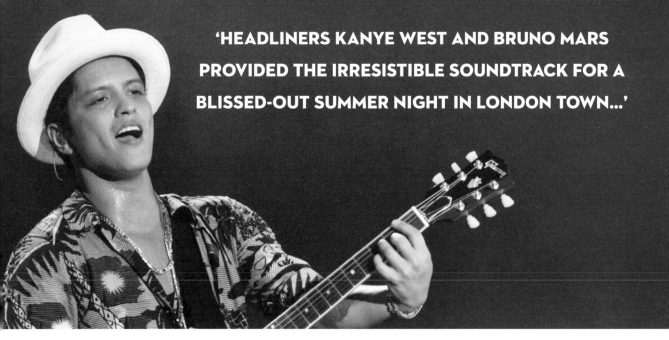

'HEADLINERS KANYE WEST AND BRUNO MARS PROVIDED THE IRRESISTIBLE SOUNDTRACK FOR A BLISSED-OUT SUMMER NIGHT IN LONDON TOWN...'

event, as well as hear it; I don't want to be able to hear people five rows behind me. That has and will always be a problem for any event held in Hyde Park or any other city centre or residential area, and that is apparently one of the reasons behind Live Nation moving the festival from Hyde Park to Finsbury Park in 2014. The issue was brought into focus in 2012 when Bruce Springsteen and the E-Street Band headlined the second night of the 'Hard Rock Calling' concert in Hyde Park. Towards the end of the gig they welcomed a special guest onto the stage – a certain Sir Paul McCartney – for whom the crowd went absolutely crazy, myself included! Both the Boss and Macca love to perform, and when they do, they take to the stage for as long as they want. So whoever made the decision to 'pull the plug' on these musical legends after the show overran for 30 minutes deserves, if anything, some kind of 'jobs worth' badge. Even if it was the local council…

Learning a valuable lesson, Wireless decamped and set its foundations in Finsbury Park in north London, a park that has a great history with live music with other festivals and bands enjoying the surroundings. From hosting Morrissey in 1992, Bob Dylan in 1993, Oasis and New Order in 2002, through to The Stone Roses in 2013 and Arctic Monkeys in 2014, north London's finest green space is an ideal venue for such a prestigious live event. This could be the beginning of a beautiful partnership and maybe – just maybe – Wireless might have guitar bands back and crank the voume upto 11!

Above: Bruno Mars headlined the 2014 Wireless Festival.

FIELD DAY –
VICTORIA PARK, JUNE

Field Day also takes place in Victoria Park, normally before Lovebox, in June. Year on year, since it began in 2007, the festival has expanded and sold out each time. It's a real personal passion for its organiser and music-loving festival maverick Tom Baker, who pays attention to every minuscule detail to make sure his festival not only succeeds but also lives up to both his own and his punters' lofty expectations. Baker set up his own promotion company, 'Eat Your Own Ears', in 2001 and has worked with a variety of artists very early on in their careers, including Anthony and the Johnsons, Florence and the Machine, The XX and Danger Mouse. He also programmes one-off shows and produces groundbreaking events that are purely aimed at showcasing and highlighting great new music, and set up Field Day to reflect this cross section of genre-defining artists. The festival has a very eclectic mix of artists and has a reputation for booking some very interesting and unheard of acts, many of which other curators wouldn't even think about

booking. What other mainstream festival has booked Ginger Baker's Jazz Confusion or the mighty Thurston Moore?

This eclectic roster of artists (and perhaps its close proximity to trendy east London) draws quite a hipster crowd, but I love how the organisers try to out-hipster even the hippest of hipster by throwing in a few obscure artists from a far-flung corner of the world. Tom Baker is very aware of the growing market place and the competition year on year to book the right acts and sell enough tickets to survive. Being unique is what he believes keeps Field Day ahead of the game and makes it stand out from the evergrowing crowd of music festivals – by not booking bands that are playing every event under the sun, but digging deep to find those bands that might not have played for a number of years (such as Ginger Baker), a debut artist, or even an artist from the most obscure corner of the musical establishment. It is about challenging and stimulating an audience that is enthusiastic and open-minded in equal measure.

The stages and tents are named after various venues and club nights, including Tom's very own 'Eat Your Own Ears' label. There's also the 'Bugged Out' stage, a performance area dedicated to one of the longest-running UK club nights, which recently celebrated its 20th birthday.

Bugged Out have their own weekender, which takes place out of normal festival season, normally in January. The Shacklewell Arms is not only an important partner of the festival but is instrumental to the live music scene in east London. The pub, based in Dalston, is renowned for showcasing the next big thing and has become the place to go if you want to see the latest bands and artists make their live debut. It has been around for about 25 years and has seen The Horrors, Ariel Pink and Solange play, amongst many, many others.

Playing is almost secondary to many bands that grace the stages of Field Day; many of them cite a list of bands on the bill they have either seen or are about to go and watch. That's quite a different attitude from other festivals, and a healthy one too. Indeed Field Day has become the 'artists' festival – a showcase of the contemporary and progressive, with prestige at both the top and the bottom of its splendid bill. What's more, Field Day is a great supporter of War Child – which seems like a perfect partnership between such an enduring charity and such a progressive live music event.

As soon as you enter Field Day's site, even on the walk there from the Overground (or whatever form of transport you end up taking) the enthusiasm and energy is infectious. There is a real feeling of excitement about seeing something I've never seen before – about discovering something I've never heard of or being swayed to an artist that I was convinced wasn't really my bag. It's not the kind of festival where you search out your favourite band. Tom Baker believes it's a great time for music and people being open to new and different genres of music. When asked if Field Day had a personality, what would that personality be, he said, 'someone who is open-minded and has eclectic taste, loves different genres of music and is also quite serious but also completely up for letting go and having a fun, hedonistic time.'

Field Day is indeed a fantastic opportunity to see some wonderful live music if you are visiting London this summer, or if you live in London and have people come to stay. Every music genre is covered in some way, shape or form, and if you live in London it encourages you to take that festival spirit to your local park. That is probably one of the other things I take for granted living in such a fantastic metropolis – you forget and ignore the things that are within easy reach. There's so much great live music – it's almost unreal.

'THE FESTIVAL HAS A VERY ECLECTIC MIX OF ARTISTS AND HAS A REPUTATION FOR BOOKING SOME VERY INTERESTING AND UNHEARD OF ACTS.'

FIEL

Tate/Etsy
Craft Tent

VILLAGE
GREEN

Venn Street
Market

M

RED STRIPE
BANDSTAND

RED BULL MUSIC
ACADEMY

London
Brewers
Market

MAIN
ENTRANCE

BOX OFFICES

*Field Day takes place
in London's Victoria
Park in June.*

Janelle Monáe
prepares to rock
the Latitude faithful
in 2012.

WHERE: *Suffolk*   **WHEN:** *Mid July*

LATITUDE

Most likely to see: Richard Curtis and his family
getting their faces painted by the Pimm's Tent.

Scan here to see Edith's
Latitude essentials.

Latitude is still quite a new and young festival but one that very much knows its place and what it stands for. Set in the opulent Henham Park near Southwold in Suffolk, the festival began life in 2006 with a capacity of 20,000. Part of the Festival Republic family, Latitude compliments its Reading, Leeds and Electric Picnic relatives by continually maintaining its critical appeal. It takes place over a weekend in the middle of July, which should give it the benefit of fine weather – although it's Britain and the

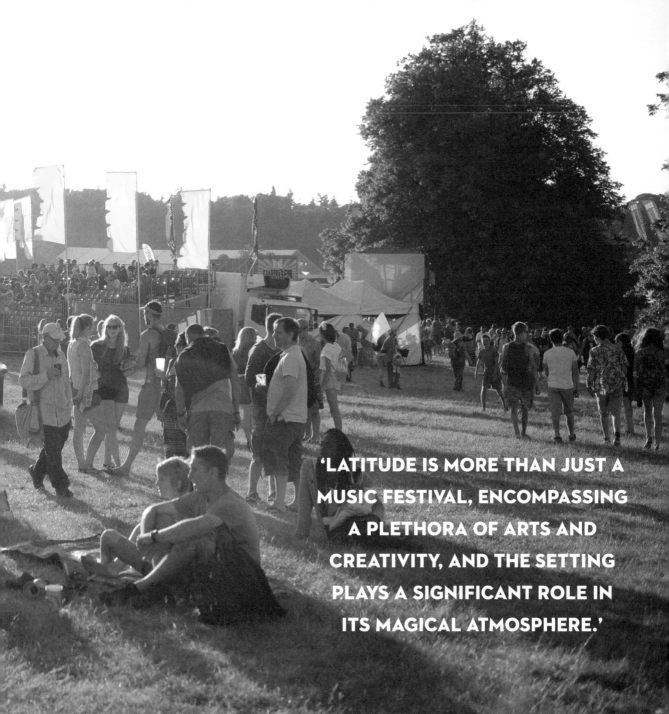

weather is something we can never rely on, festival or no festival! In fact Latitude has dealt with almost monsoon conditions in its short life, and you'll be happy to read that no performances have been cancelled and the twinkly lights have survived.

Latitude is very similar to Glastonbury, but on a much smaller scale. Like its Somerset counterpart, it's more than just a music festival, encompassing a plethora of arts and creativity, and the setting, just like the festival on

'LATITUDE IS MORE THAN JUST A MUSIC FESTIVAL, ENCOMPASSING A PLETHORA OF ARTS AND CREATIVITY, AND THE SETTING PLAYS A SIGNIFICANT ROLE IN ITS MAGICAL ATMOSPHERE.'

Worthy Farm, plays a significant role in the magical atmosphere of Latitude. The beautiful former hunting grounds of Henham Park in Suffolk are an amazing backdrop to what is a real favourite with punters on the festival circuit. From the lovely lakes at the southern end of the park, to the pastel-painted sheep, Latitude, like Glasto, is a very popular festival that is truly British in outlook: the green, lush Suffolk countryside protects and cuddles the site, with the seaside only a few miles away; the campsites are strewn upwards across a number of verdant fields and separated from the main arena by the lake and snake-like forest. It really is a glorious site, and although not quite having the glamorous history of British stalwart Glastonbury, it still maintains a sense of mystique and of originality.

Indeed one of Latitude's major selling points is its family-friendly vibe. Unlike some of the more 'raucous' festivals (such as Reading or Leeds), Latitude prides itself on attracting a largely middle-class audience, with its focus not only on music, poetry and creative arts, but also on kid-centric events and family fun. It is thus viewed as one of the 'safer' festivals on the circuit and families tend to allow their kids to bolt off and play in the musical 'playground', while mum and dad catch up with the world on a nearby 'park bench'. Only the kids are off watching Rudimental, while mum and dad get drunk and cry their eyes out during Dexys Midnight Runners' set! With most festivals you could just turn up without any luggage or sleeping equipment as the rise in boutique camping at festivals has become a necessity as opposed to a luxury.

Culture, colour and creativity are at the core of the Latitude idyll: there really is something for everyone – kids, mums and dads, and even old age pensioners! The festival transcends generations and there's a real community spirit to every nook and cranny of the festival ground. Walking amongst the colourful grounds of Henham Park on the Saturday morning is like being at an elaborate village fete with food and drink stalls, a helter-skelter, circus tents, and even a piano garden! Latitude is like an 'enchanted forest', with lakes and woodland kissing the outskirts of the main arena that themselves offer a plethora of stimulation – from secret stages nestled under the canopy of an overgrown oak tree, to the twinkling lights of the hidden-away I-Arena at dusk.

'FROM THE LOVELY LAKES AT THE SOUTHERN END OF THE PARK, TO THE PASTEL-PAINTED SHEEP, LATITUDE, LIKE GLASTO, IS A VERY POPULAR FESTIVAL THAT IS TRULY BRITISH IN OUTLOOK.'

The managing director of Festival Republic, Melvin Benn, started the festival as an indulgence to look at and explore all the diverse aspects of art and culture that he enjoyed. It's a festival that couldn't have existed 30 years ago but according to Melvin, 'it was needed, it was needed for me to break the mould. I wanted to create a festival not just for people who had music as the only thing in their lives. My cultural development had begun and I started to be interested in opera, the arts and it came about because of that and it's a joy.' The incredible diversity is something Latitude has offered from the very beginning and is one of the reasons it has grown to be one of the most important and loved festivals on the circuit in such a short space of time.

LATITUDE: THE CULTURE AND THE MUSIC

Audiences are encouraged to be brave at Latitude and are given the opportunity to enhance their viewing and listening habits more so than at many other festivals. Expectations are left at home as festival goers can take the time to experience productions that might be deemed unattainable or unpopular for the mainstream. Unlike a number of other festivals, the theatre, poetry and dance tents see huge crowds, captivated and delighted by what's on offer: there's the wonderful Live Art tent nestled in the corner of the park's woodland, and the Royal Shakespeare Company also set up camp; film-makers answer questions in front of a live audience inside the Film tent in the heart of the site, while children can marvel in the science tent or visit the on-site library.

Yet Latitude is a still a music festival and there is plenty of music on offer. Weaved into the trees are small performance areas which really add something unquestionable to the experience. These small stages almost don't feel like stages – they're more performance 'platforms', allowing you to get so close to the bands and artists you sometimes feel like you are on stage with them.

Some festivals really suffer with noise exposure between stages and there really is nothing worse than sound bleeding from one stage or tent into another. This isn't the case at Henham Park: I'm not sure if there has been some kind of environmental experiment conducted into wind and sound movement at the Southwold site, but the audio from each sound stage

'UNLIKE A NUMBER OF OTHER FESTIVALS, THE THEATRE, POETRY AND DANCE TENTS SEE HUGE CROWDS, CAPTIVATED AND DELIGHTED BY WHAT'S ON OFFER...'

is locked to that stage and doesn't filter through. That might sound like an inconsequential observation but there is nothing more annoying than trying to listen to a band at a festival when you can hear the sound coming from a tent not too far away. Much like sitting next to someone on public transport who is listening to music just a little too loud for their own good, and you have no choice but to endure it!

Latitude is, first and foremost, a music festival, and I have always felt the organisation is incredibly supportive of new music, especially bands on the brink of bigger and better things. From providing one of the aforementioned 'performance platforms' to an unknown solo artist, to offering a headline slot to a relatively new band, Latitude shows trust and offers a real 'you can do it' mentality to all of their performers. From spending time backstage I've noticed a real air of relaxation amongst artists and a genuine feeling of being happy to be there and be part of something. Egos, thankfully, seem to have been left on the A12 motorway back towards London.

The festival is also conscious of getting hold of established talent of the music industry and reminding them of their brilliance, like Patti Smith in its inaugural year in 2006, which was only the start of a typically decorated roster. Indeed, Festival Republic Managing Director Melvin Benn has been on record saying Arcade Fire, who closed the main stage in 2007, are probably the band that totally represents the festival: Arcade Fire's

combination of music and art, and their multitude of influences reflects Latitude's approach to its creative output – a desire to challenge, inspire and stimulate.

Other glorious bookings include Damon Albarn, who has played the festival in various guises over the years. The Good, The Bad and The Queen headlined on the Saturday night back in 2007, a spot he revisited with his Heavy Seas in 2014, with the added bonus of Blur band mate Graham Coxon joining him on stage for a truly magical rendition of 'Tender'. In fact, my first ever experience of the festival was in 2009, waking up on site after making my way down to Suffolk on a tour bus to the sleepy realisation that Thom Yorke would be opening the main stage on the Sunday morning – a stage that would later be headlined by Nick Cave and the Bad Seeds. The Radiohead frontman had every right to play anything he wanted – it was just him and his acoustic guitar, after all. No one expected him to play any Radiohead stuff, but we never imagined he would sprinkle his 12-track set with six Radiohead songs including 'Follow Me Around' and 'There There'.

DJ and festival guru Huw Stephens, who has been curating the Lake Stage since the very first Latitude after he asked Melvin if he needed a DJ for the inaugural year, gets the chance to not only book some of the most exciting new bands on the circuit for the festival, but also books musicians and performers who don't always play festivals. It also gives him a chance to see things he hasn't seen before: 'I go to gigs, a lot of gigs. I always see something amazing at Latitude – a poet I'd never see otherwise, a comedian, or someone like "Mr Bingo", who sends artistic and abusive postcards to people. There's a special, hungry attitude there that I love; everyone is there for the arts as a whole.'

Huw was responsible for booking Metronomy and Friendly Fires back in 2007, Bombay Bicycle Club and The XX in 2009, James Blake and Ghostpoet in 2011 and Sam Smith and The 1975

> **'I ALWAYS SEE SOMETHING AMAZING AT LATITUDE - A POET I'D NEVER SEE OTHERWISE, A COMEDIAN, OR SOMEONE LIKE "MR BINGO", WHO SENDS ARTISTIC AND ABUSIVE POSTCARDS TO PEOPLE.' — HUW STEVENS**

in 2013. The Lake Stage has most definitely been a breeding ground for bands and artists to then go on to bigger and better things, so if you were lucky enough to see these giants of music in such an intimate setting, give yourself a pat on the back!

NAVIGATING LATITUDE

Latitude is a relatively new festival and not much has changed since it started in 2006. The audience has grown since its inception but I find it comforting that the festival organisers increased the arena size in 2012, not to pull in a bigger crowd but to open the space up and make more room for those already there. It also meant the building of a second bridge across the lake, partly due to the success of a particular performance of *Swan Lake* that caused gridlock on the bridge!

It's a really easy site to navigate and one that you can get round

*Graham Coxon joined his old band mate
Damon Albarn on stage for a rendition of the
Blur song 'Tender' in 2014. It was a special
moment in what was a very special set.*

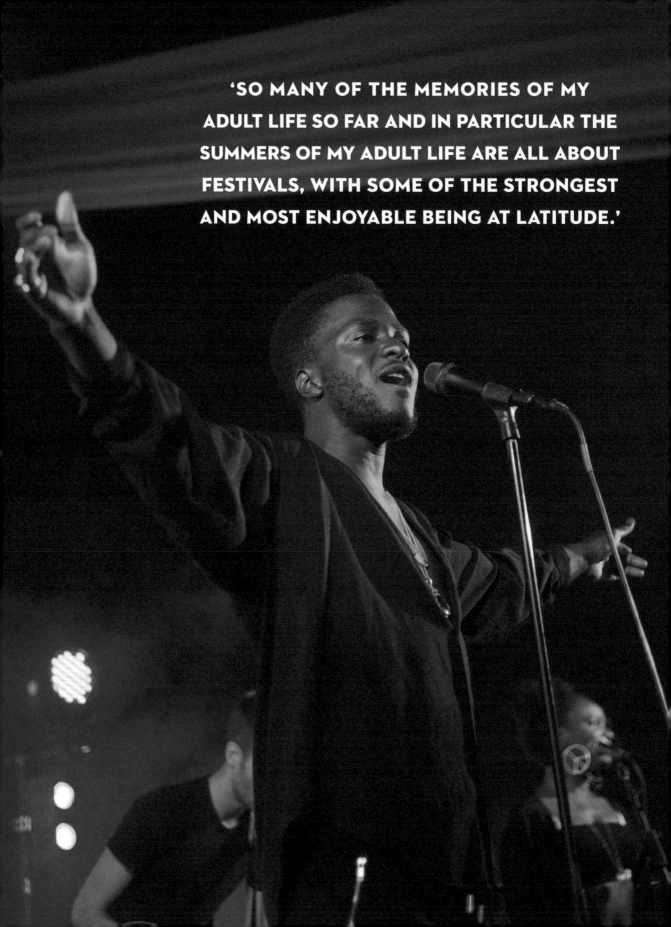

'SO MANY OF THE MEMORIES OF MY ADULT LIFE SO FAR AND IN PARTICULAR THE SUMMERS OF MY ADULT LIFE ARE ALL ABOUT FESTIVALS, WITH SOME OF THE STRONGEST AND MOST ENJOYABLE BEING AT LATITUDE.'

pretty quickly. This is a good thing for someone like me who always tries to achieve more than is physically possible. I can be seen first thing in the morning with a festival guide and a highlighter pen, marking out my plans for the day, allowing the odd break for discovery. But there are some festivals where the line-up is just so good you want to see a bit of everything. I seem to have a romantic notion that I have some kind of transportation device that will beam me from stage to stage. Latitude is actually a pretty good size should you wish to attempt to break the world record for 'most bands seen in one day' – even the stages tucked away behind a cluster of ash and oak trees.

Space – and room to move around – isn't something that you expect when you are at a festival, but at Latitude there is plenty of it. In fact, I feel like I'm in some kind of soft focus advert as I meander through clouds of colourful stimuli, slowly making my way to the next live performance area. Latitude doesn't seem interested in growing year on year or facilitating any notion of becoming bigger than it needs to be. It maintains that personal and attentive nature of a smaller and younger festival, which makes it all the more successful and necessary.

Getting to Latitude does take an element of planning and commitment, unless of course you live in Southwold or the surrounding countryside. I'd suggest finding the nearest camper van, stocking up on friends and supplies, and pitching up on site on the Thursday night. If you are flying solo and looking for a cheap travel option or if you have spare seats in your car then you should really get in touch with BlaBlaCar – a European rideshare network, which is a bit like pre-arranged hitchhiking! It can guarantee you access to a priority car park right outside the main festival entrance; it's also cheaper than the train and if you give a couple of people a lift it will have covered your travel costs... A win-win situation! There are other options, of course; you can get there by coach, foot, taxi and bike or even by air (let's not forget that Norwich International Airport is only up the A146!).

Alternatively why not apply to be a cat, hat or pixie? These are the names given to the volunteer stewards who, when on site, can answer any questions you might have and help you carry your belongings or pitch your tent. I was assisted by one particular pixie in the summer of 2014 who drove me across a small lake to the iArena nestled in a truly atmospheric woodland setting to watch Kwabs. That was the archetypal Latitude experience!

Left: The archetypal Latitude experience: I took a boat across a lake to catch Kwabs... it was so worth it!

My husband Tom Smith performs with his band Editors at the 2014 edition of Latitude (I'm trying to stay out of sight to not put him off!).

A FESTIVAL OF MEMORIES

Scan here to listen to Sharleen Spiteri's reflections on festivals and Latitude.

Latitude is a festival I have grown into and I really look forward to going back year after year. I think that's helped by the fact I've been able to attend the festival in various guises for various reasons – whether that be through work, such as when I got to interview the incredible Abi Morgan about her work as a screenwriter and playwright in the BAFTA tent, or be the supportive wife to my husband Tom when his band Editors played over the years, or just go with friends and have another memorable British summer festival experience. I love nothing better than watching a band with my other half, especially at a festival. It was something we did at the very start of our relationship and something we still do regularly, whether he is playing or not. So many of the memories of my adult life so far and in particular the summers of my adult life are all about festivals, with some of the strongest and most enjoyable being at Latitude. I like the intimacy of it, the familiarity of it and the easiness of it. But I think what I like about it best is the musical choices it makes.

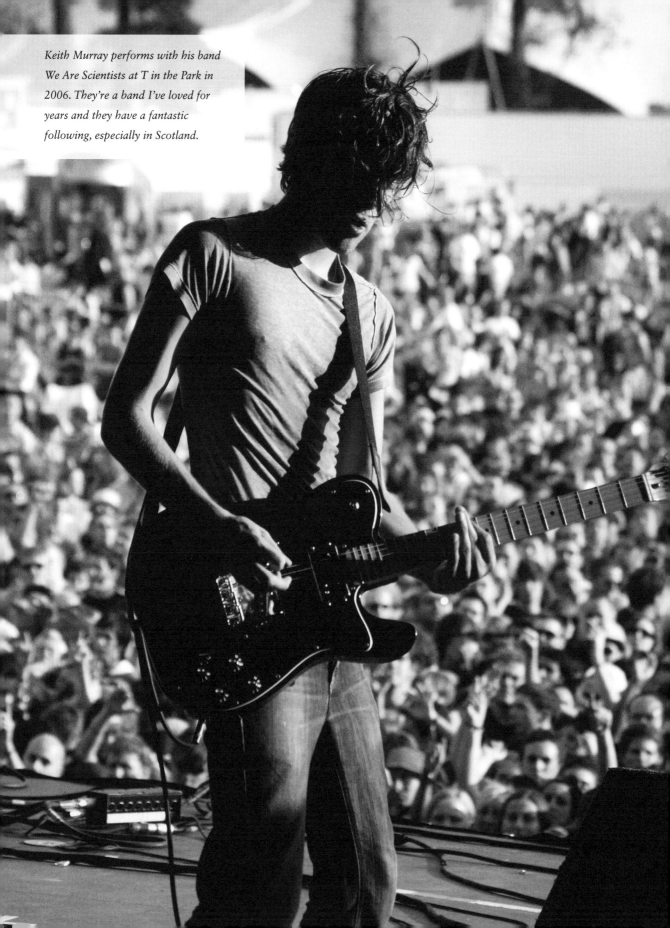

Keith Murray performs with his band
We Are Scientists at T in the Park in
2006. They're a band I've loved for
years and they have a fantastic
following, especially in Scotland.

WHERE: *Perthshire, Scotland* **WHEN:** *Second weekend of July*

T IN THE PARK

Most likely to see: At least one person with horrendous sunburn, even though there's been torrential rain for the entire weekend.

Scan here to see Edith's T essentials.

Back in 1994 there was only Glastonbury, Reading and Womad; Green Man was yet to appear on the horizon of the Black Mountains of Abergavenny, and Bestival was but a twinkle in Rob Da Bank's eye. Scotland, meanwhile, was missing out on all the fun, and by the middle of the 1990s festival enthusiasts north of the border decided it was about time that it had its own major yearly music celebration – after all Scotland not only has an impressive musical heritage but the Scottish audience is second to none. There was the odd one-day project that popped up here and there but nothing to fulfil the wants and needs of a music-hungry race year on year. And so T in the Park was born.

T in the Park is part of Scotland's heritage; it's a huge publicity pull for the country and it really does the country proud. It also showcases the raw energy and enthusiasm of a Scottish music-loving fan – ie me! This is the festival that I have the most history with – my initiation, my first. It's also the one I've been to the most and where I became hooked on the want and need to be part of the music festival experience.

THE HISTORY OF T IN THE PARK

T started in 1994, originally in Strathclyde Park with 18,000 people attending each day over a weekend at the end of July. It was, if you didn't already know, named after its main sponsor, the brewing company Tennent's who actually started the venture with DF Concerts. Originally the sponsors were interested in hosting a big, one-off outdoor event, but were convinced otherwise by the promoters that there was potential for a series of live events. The festival moved to Balado airfield in Kinross-shire in 1997 purely because it outgrew Strathclyde Park. Then in 2015 it moved to the grounds of the 19th century Strathallan Castle, Perthshire, due to concerns about health and safety around the underground oil pipeline on the Balado site.

Geoff Ellis, the festival's founder, has been the 'Don Corleone' of the festival from the very start (making bands offers they simply cannot refuse!) and his passion for great music and great bands is at the heart of T in the Park and its appeal. He has quite a history too: an adopted Scot who moved to Glasgow in 1992, Geoff is manager of King Tut's Wah Wah Hut, still one of the most legendary and important venues in the country. Geoff's reputation is an integral part of the 'T in the Park' brand, and his contact book allows the festival to compete against its English and Welsh counterparts year after

'T IN THE PARK IS PART OF SCOTLAND'S HERITAGE; IT'S A HUGE PUBLICITY PULL FOR THE COUNTRY AND IT REALLY DOES THE COUNTRY PROUD.'

year after year. It's also one of the reasons the festival's numbers tripled in the first ten or so years: by 2003 it was attracting crowds of 55,000 each day.

Today the festival attracts 85,000, making it the second largest festival in the UK and fifth largest in the world in terms of attendance. Twenty-five per cent of the crowd is made up of visitors from outside Scotland, with about two per cent attending from overseas (I love a stat, don't you?). Of course, being the size it is and attracting those

kinds of numbers means building strong and loyal relationships with those who live close by is a necessity. This is something the festival excels at: it had very strong relationships with the local community in and around Balado during its stint there and I'm sure it will maintain strong links with the local community once it moves to Strathallan in Perthshire in 2015. A festival would not be able to survive a few years, let alone 18 years, without building great and trusting friendships with locals – which is something that the festival has had to do time and time again. What other festivals have moved site, not just once but three times in 20 years? The new site is 14 miles west of Balado, so is still accessible to the whole of Scotland and is a prettier site with a castle, more woodland, more aesthetics to play with.

As mentioned, T in the Park was originally a two-day event but in 2007 bands started to play on the Friday, from late afternoon onwards. Lily Allen, replete in ball gown, trainers and rain poncho, was the first to play the Friday night, while Arctic Monkeys were given the job of headlining the first three-day event. This maintained a roster of wonderful acts who have played the festival since its inception in 1994: Rage Against the Machine, Blur, Paul Weller, Radiohead, and Pulp all made appearances between 1994 and 2003; Flaming Lips,

The Prodigy, Arctic Monkeys, Beyoncé, Coldplay and Foo Fighters have all made appearances at the bonnie party thereafter.

And that's exactly what it is – a massive party that celebrates and revels in the Scottish performing arts scene, taking place in a wonderful location at the height of a Gaelic summer. Thus it wasn't a surprise when the organisers teamed up with Oxegen Festival – Ireland's own muddy extravaganza – which takes place over the same weekend at Punchestown Racecourse, County Kildare in Ireland. In recent years the two festivals have shared lineups, with acts appearing on alternate nights at each festival.

'T IS A MASSIVE PARTY THAT CELEBRATES THE SCOTTISH PERFORMING ARTS SCENE, TAKING PLACE IN A WONDERFUL LOCATION AT THE HEIGHT OF A GAELIC SUMMER.'

T TODAY

What has kept T alive for over 20 years and allowed it to remain hugely successful within that time? Geoff Ellis, the festival director, believes a successful festival has to create a unique opportunity for the audience and whilst he might have someone who has been coming for over twenty years, he might also have someone coming for the first time; it's therefore his responsibility to try and make it relevant to both those fans, and everyone in between.

The key is to therefore keep the festival as fresh as possible. T in the Park's frequent relocations – from Strathclyde Park to Balado to Strathallan – has given the organisers opportunities to take stock and make alterations to suit the site, and also re-evaluate its standing on the festival calendar; it has also given its audience the opportunity to provide their own feedback – particularly about the music and the various activities on offer at the site. T in the Park has thus remained at the forefront of the Scottish music scene by listening to its audience, freshening up and moving with the times – both literally and figuratively.

Right: Alex Turner of the Arctic Monkeys before he went all swagger on us. He is one of my favourite front men and I love everything he does! Here he is on stage for the Arctic's first ever appearance at T in 2006...

A moment of contemplation for The Streets' Mike Skinner, performing in front of a packed King Tut's tent at T in the Park.

Every relocation is a huge amount of work for the organisers, and as the new site of Strathallan welcomes T and its music-loving carousers, they have had to once again plan and clear the site's layout, traffic management, licence applications – and that's before they think about tickets, bands, and, of course, camping. A brand new framework for each location requires a lot of work and patience.

The new site of Strathallan Castle should provide T with the award for one of the most beautiful sites for a UK festival. Auchterarder is the nearest town to the site (I'm really looking forward to listening to non-Scots trying to pronounce that one! I can already hear it now: 'Octerardor'... 'Actorerdar'!), and located within an hour of Glasgow and Edinburgh, amongst the most glorious and rich Scottish countryside. With over 1,000 acres of land to host the scores of music-loving fans, the site is overlooked by the castle, which acts as a fantastic natural amphitheatre and lends itself beautifully to the main stage. Although it isn't a boutique festival, the new site will definitely allow elements of a boutique festival to

be explored. The festival began with two main stages, along with the Caledonian Stage to showcase up and coming new bands. The dance tent was added in 1995, later to be transformed into what has now become synonymous with the T set-up, The Slam Tent – a legend in its own right which plays host to some of the most talented DJs in the world. Today the main stage is flanked by King Tut's Wah Wah tent and the Radio 1/NME stage at the front of the site, while the Slam Tent pops up just before the camping area begins in the northern part of the site. The new site also makes it easier to move between stages and navigate your way around the site, with tree-lined avenues making natural roadways between the two main stages.

T in the Park has always seemed untouchable and has survived many highs and lows. They deliberately decided against the Glastonbury-style ticket registration as the organisers felt it would cause an inconvenience for their punters. Yes, it would cut down on ticket touting but it would be more difficult to get tickets for those who have been supporters of the festival and might want to come back.

Scan here to listen to Twin Atlantic's memories of T in the Park and Glastonbury…

Right: Arctic Monkeys
take to the stage...

WHO ATTENDS T?

The crowd at T in the Park is one of the best in the world. Ask any band or artist and, without a doubt, they will confirm if there is one crowd guaranteed to give it their all – whatever the weather – it's music-loving revellers of T. People are quick to define a 'T in the Park crowd' in a derogatory fashion, which is something I take major umbrage with. The crowd at T goes for it, they like to lose their inhibitions and for some it's the annual opportunity to lose themselves and have the best time possible.

I have various family members who take their annual holiday at T in the Park, and I've watched convoys of cars weave their way through Fife to Kinross packed with people, tents and trolleys for transporting their goods and supplies from the car park to the campsite. Then it's the regular updates and requests from my brother and various cousins and distant relatives about trying to meet up or, what is now an age old tradition, of calling me and holding up the phone during a specific song, even though I am either in the crowd or watching it on television!

The audience at T is very broad; a large proportion of it is aged 18–25. But Geoff Ellis says that it's not restricted to age when you talk about the audience: 'it's attitudinal, not age-specific. They are into music and they still love discovering music, they might be 45 but they feel 25.' The T crowd are the most passionate in the world – they are high octane and vociferous. 'You can only lose the audience,' remarks Texas' Sharleen Spiteri. 'You don't have to whip them up into a frenzy as they are there for you from the start. All you have to do is to keep them with you and if you lose them then you have no one to blame but yourself.

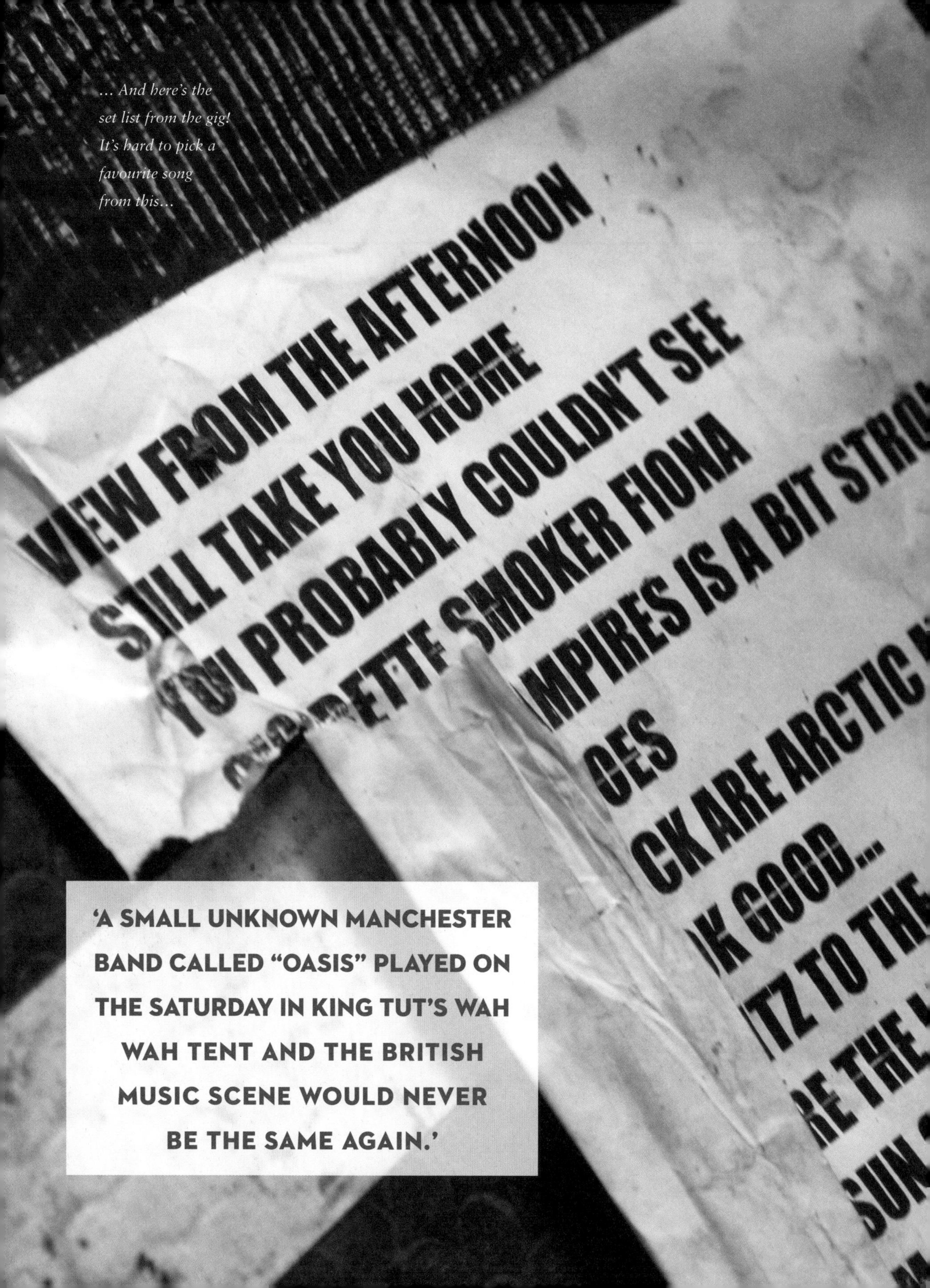

VIEW FROM THE AFTERNOON

STILL TAKE YOU HOME

YOU PROBABLY COULDN'T SEE

CIGARETTE SMOKER FIONA

VAMPIRES IS A BIT STRO

...CES

...CK ARE ARCTIC...

...K GOOD...

...TZ TO THE

...RE THE...

...SUN...

'A SMALL UNKNOWN MANCHESTER
BAND CALLED "OASIS" PLAYED ON
THE SATURDAY IN KING TUT'S WAH
WAH TENT AND THE BRITISH
MUSIC SCENE WOULD NEVER
BE THE SAME AGAIN.'

THE MUSIC

Along with the T crowd, the music policy has always been a stand out and trusted feature of T. The organisers have never shown any sign of music snobbery over the years: it's always been about providing something for everyone, as Geoff mentions earlier. From commercially successful headliners to upcoming artists, brand new and unsigned bands, ceilidhs, and those artists that have had an incredible career and might have disappeared off the radar. It's about loyalty – the organisers respect the bands and their music and celebrate what they might have achieved in the past – which is something I think a lot of other festivals won't do.

The debut headliners Blur and Rage Against The Machine are a great example of this music policy: edgy, popular and to some degree divisive, the first crop of headliners became the blueprint for all subsequent T headliners. Also in that first year a small unknown Manchester band called 'Oasis' played on the Saturday in King Tut's Wah Wah Tent and the British music scene would never be the same again. Noel has since come back to T with High Flying Birds, as has Liam with Beady Eye. Who knows, it might be the place for them to finally reunite.

Arctic Monkeys have a fantastic relationship with T. They were the first headliner when the festival became a three-day event and they were the last band to play at Balado before T moved to its new home in 2014. The festival was also part of the live resurrection of The Stone Roses in 2012, with a rather dramatic *Scotland on Sunday* noting, 'T in the Park had been waiting for this moment, not just all weekend, but since the festival's very inception in 1994.' There seems to be a big 'moment' every year at T; it is genuinely that kind of place.

There is another band that I immediately think of when T is mentioned and that's Biffy Clyro. They're a band who have said that without T in the Park they wouldn't be where they are today. They played for the first time on the T Break Stage back in 1999 after winning a competition and were duly signed. Ten years later they headlined T for the very first time, in what seemed like a fitting tribute to the festival's nurturing and promotion of fantastic local talent.

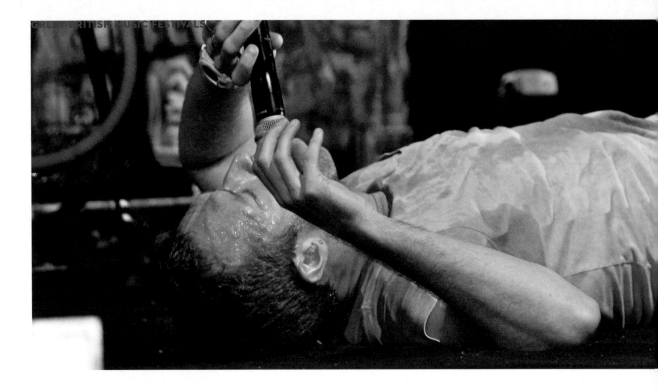

T FOR ME

As mentioned in the Introduction to this book, the first time I went to T in the Park was in 1995 and it was also my first ever festival. I was still studying in Edinburgh but managed to blag my way into a work experience placement at my local radio station. When they asked me to come along to T in the big black double-decker bus that doubled up as a studio, I felt like all my Christmases had come at once. I was there to do anything – whatever was needed to make sure we made the best radio possible. I was trusted with a large recording device and sent off to see what I could get. From the corner of my eye I spotted Kylie Minogue making her way into the backstage ladies' toilets and I thought this is my moment. I hovered outside the loos and waited to pounce. Thankfully Kylie wasn't freaked out by a young Scottish upstart with a larger than usual microphone waiting for her outside a toilet, she gave me my first ever interview and revealed to me the secret that everyone had been trying to second-guess. Who was the special guest that would take to the stage during her set on the main stage at T? No, it wasn't Jason Donovan, but the legendary and wonderful Nick Cave. Not only my first interview but an exclusive. I got a gold star!

Above: Chris Martin puts everything into it, as usual, during a performance on the main stage at T in the Park.

T has been one of those places I've been lucky enough to see most of the bands I grew up listening to and is within spitting distance of my hometown of Anstruther, which is just over an hour down the road. It was, for instance, the festival The Stone Roses chose to play their first festival in a long time – and I got to see it! It being so close to home came with certain expectations from the rather large family I am fortunate to have – including my mum who was the person to take me to my first concert when I was eight (Rod Stewart at Ibrox Stadium in Glasgow). To be able to take her to T and give her free reign to watch and listen to some of the best artists around is just one of my happiest moments and biggest achievements. However, the moment she went missing in 2006 on site was one I will never forget: as I was about to go live on TV, bigging-up our coverage on the last night of the festival with music coming up from The Strokes, Arctic Monkeys, Paul Weller, Editors and loads more, no one had any idea where she was. Nobody apart from my good friend Douglas Anderson, who was watching the performances on a small monitor in the studio. There she was, my mum at the side of stage, air tambourine in hand, centimetres from actually being on stage with Primal Scream, in her head doing backing vocals for 'Country Girl'! She is the reason I do what I do and the reason music is such a big part of my life. Never change, Mum. Thank you.

*The very brilliant
Seasick Steve.*

CAMBRIDGE FOLK FESTIVAL

WHERE: *Cambridge*   **WHEN:** *End of July / Start of August*

CAMBRIDGE FOLK FESTIVAL

Most likely to see: Lots of beards. And acoustic guitars.
In fact lots of bearded men with acoustic guitars.

Scan here to see Edith's
Cambridge essentials.

I've heard so many people enthuse about the Cambridge Folk Festival over the years and I have no logical or particular excuse as to why I've not been. It pains me to admit and I feel slightly mortified too! Folk music incorporates so many different influences, places and instrumentation. One of the great misconceptions around the Cambridge Folk Festival for those who haven't been is that it's purely one type of music and this is a misconception I hope to expose and explore in the following pages.

When I think of the Cambridge Folk Festival it reminds me of my professional guiding light, Mark Radcliffe, who I've been lucky enough to know for years. He couldn't have been more encouraging and supportive when I started at BBC Radio 1; I also worked with him at Glastonbury and he gave me staunch advice on writing this book. He has spent the last 10 years broadcasting for both radio and TV from the Cambridge Folk Festival and has spent many years watching some of his favourite artists and bands and discovering an enormous collection of new ones.

Mark Radcliffe was therefore the perfect person to speak to about its history, why he thinks it has managed to survive the test of musical times, and what he adores about the festival that draws him back year after year.

'Cambridge has become one of the events that I just look forward to as part of summer,' says Mark. 'It always feels like a bit of a homecoming and it's terribly civilised, they even played *The Archers* over the main stage PA on Sunday lunchtime, whilst everyone got their travelling rugs out and read the papers, so very English. But the music is truly international and part of the charm of the festival is that you feel the history of the event as it's always been in the same place. That chimes well with the folk scene; tradition is such a massive part of it all. Innovation is a huge part of the scene too, but the folkies really respect their history. That and how they listen to music. There is a very particular way of listening at a folk festival; the audience listen to every word, they pay attention.'

'ONE OF THE GREAT MISCONCEPTIONS AROUND THE CAMBRIDGE FOLK FESTIVAL FOR THOSE WHO HAVEN'T BEEN IS THAT IT'S PURELY ONE TYPE OF MUSIC.'

Van Morrison performs at Cherry Hinton Hall in 2014.

FROM NEWPORT TO CAMBRIDGE: A HISTORY

The Cambridge Folk Festival is one of the longest-running and most famous folk festivals in the world, and in 2014 it celebrated its 50th anniversary. But how did it get to such an impressive point? Back in 1964, Cambridge City Council set about planning a music event for the following year and approached Ken Woollard, a local firefighter and political activist, to take the reigns. Woollard was a visionary who avoided public attention at all counts. He was also a man who had no particular musical talent of his own but who quite clearly saw the existing and potential talent in others. The first festival went ahead in 1965 and, as part of the organising committee, Woollard was instrumental in encouraging within the festival the cross-breeding of styles and genres to promote folk music to the world. His enthusiasm was infectious and after a solid opening edition of the folk event, Cambridge City Council decided to hold an annual event with Woollard at the helm.

Woollard continued as organiser and artistic director for nearly 30 editions of the festival until his sad passing in 1993. But his legacy was well established by then: when putting together the original festival, he drew inspiration from a documentary about the 1958 Newport Jazz Festival in Rhode Island, USA, which focused primarily on the performances and audience at that festival. The Newport Festival demonstrated the importance of location and setting during live performance – both of which are integral parts of the mood and ambience at any festival (*see* chapters on Green Man and Glastonbury, amongst others). When watching the documentary about Newport you get a sense that there was a very thin line between the festival and where everyday life took over in the town and adjacent neighbourhoods. The music is circumferential of the surrounding area: people driving down the streets listening to jazz, with double basses and other instruments protruding out of the roofs of their cars; picnics in the park listening to all manner of jazz legends, and all ages watching on from deckchairs as the sun blasts incredible colour-scapes across the various sites. It was like a soundtrack to the city.

The Cambridge Folk Festival

Above: Amadou and Mariam perform at the festival in 2013.

has maintained this outlook ever since its inception; the locations are carefully chosen to suit whatever type of music is being performed – from mainstream Americana to obscure Chinese folk. Since 1965 the festival has been located in Cherry Hinton Hall, a beautiful arena owned and managed by Cambridge City Council. It has a fascinating history. Once the home of the Lord Mayor of London in the 1870s, the hall was built by John Oakes, who cut channels from external streams to create ornamental lakes throughout the gardens. It was also the location of an area known as the Giant's Grave – the resting place of the giant Gogmagog, which local folklore says lived nearby. Such personal and environmental investment very much mirrors the ethos of the festival and what it stands for.

Furthermore, Ken Woollard's aim was to establish a festival that set out the ideals of an emerging and evolving music scene, with a long-term goal of maintaining its values and showing particular loyalty to the local folk clubs. The Cambridge Festival has been described as friendly, eclectic and organised and that was one of the most important things for Ken – for it to have a family-friendly atmosphere.

The first year saw fewer than 1,500 attend the festival and it almost broke even, from a financial point of view. Since then, year on year the festival has grown in popularity and numbers, and now reaches approximately 10,000 folk fans per day. The influx of folk-heads the world over – particularly in the 1970s when thousands of people flocked to the city to check out the latest songsmiths – forced the festival to consider relocating to a bigger site, but Woollard stuck to his guns and resisted the temptation to take it to another level. His argument was based on the idea that it would lose its identity and charm – plus the festival's setting of Cherry Hinton works as a natural regulator due to the park accommodating a certain number of people. The festival thus cannot get any bigger but maintains an

invaluable sense of intimacy and inclusion (both of which are rather rare at nationwide festivals these days!).

One of the names on the line-up in the first year had just released a wonderful folk track called *I Am A Rock*. The artist, Paul Simon, was paid £15 to perform at the festival – worth about £250 today. Folklore (sorry I couldn't resist) has it that Ken would offer an artist a particular fee for playing – and they could take it or leave it. If they so much as tried to haggle with him, he'd put the phone down. Such was the reputation of the festival that more often than not they would take it. And so began the great roster of names that have played this wonderful festival, right up to the likes of Van Morrison and Sinead O'Connor in 2014.

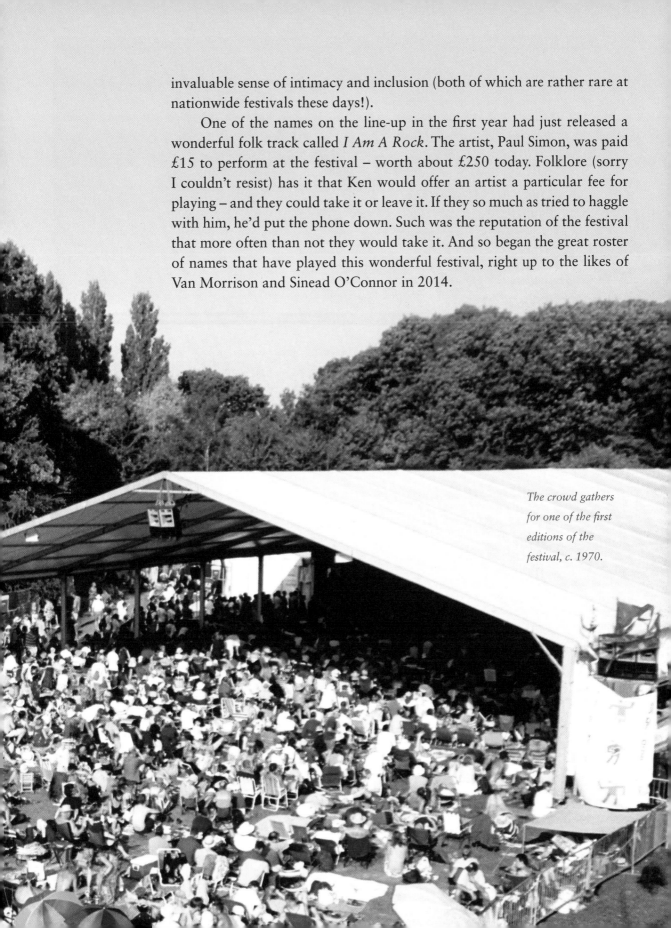

The crowd gathers for one of the first editions of the festival, c. 1970.

Laura Marling plays the main stage back in 2011.

CAMBRIDGE TODAY

Since Ken Woollard passed away in 1993 the festival has been run and programmed by Eddie Barcan, who was Ken's assistant for three years. Eddie not only shares the same philosophy from the early days but also pushes the boundaries of what is expected of the festival. It's still very much a family festival and you'll find as much music wandering around the site as you might if planted in front of the main stage for the day. One regular that I spoke to said their favourite memories of the festival aren't 'so much what was going on – on the main stage

– as with the folk club area where people, like Arlo Guthrie, just turned up. And famous names who had just performed on stage, very often came and sat in on sessions.' Indeed, the festival has built a reputation on those impromptu performances and it's almost expected of artists to make more than one appearance at the festival. Recently they have combined social media with these mysterious gigs. The 2014 edition saw the introduction of 'Tweet-outs' – secret gigs that you could only find out about if you were following the festival on Twitter or Facebook, which very much caters for the younger-end of the audience who make up a larger portion than probably expected of the festival.

Mark Radcliffe says that the first thing that struck him about the festival was how small it is: 'Cambridge really does feel like a village fete. It's not even small, about 10,000 punters, but because the main campsite at Colder's Common is away from the main site, the actual festival feels really intimate.' It is a small festival but it's not so small that it doesn't feel like a substantial event. It has never stopped moving forward and developing, ardently striving for new ideas and features. And although small in size, the festival has been thundering ahead for years in the 'influential' stakes. Over the past decade in particular there has been a huge growth in awareness and popularity of the festival, including great reviews and national television and radio coverage. But more importantly 'word of mouth' has spread, and the power of personal recommendation should not be taken for granted, especially when music and festivals are concerned.

The festival normally runs over four days at the end of July or the beginning of August. Its close proximity to the city centre gives festival goers access to all the local amenities and allows the non-camping clientele to indulge in a little home comfort without the need to deviate too far from the music areas. Cambridge, especially being a university city, is incredibly easy to access from all corners of the UK. Trains have direct links to London and other parts of the UK and it also has its own little airport should you wish to fly from selected parts of Europe and the UK.

The festival has various partnerships linked to creative needs, all of which are considered and fitting with the ethos and history of the festival. Recently a sponsorship deal with Creative Scotland has proved incredibly successful. Creative Scotland is a publicly funded organisation that has a similar role to the Arts Council. It covers performing arts, media and film, and more recently has set up an organisation to assist folk and acoustic musicians, and is tied in with the sponsorship of the Club Tent at Cambridge. The Club Tent is a more intimate acoustic environment, which houses regional folk clubs who present some of their regular performers (plus one or two guest spots from some of the big names who feature on either Stage One or Two). The festival also selects five showcase artists to appear in the Club Tent as a way of supporting new talent; the acts then also have the opportunity of appearing on the main bill the following year. Nick Mulvey, Emma Sweeney, Lucy Ward and Keston Cobblers Club have all appeared at the Club Tent stage in recent years.

In 2015 the festival will for the first time be run by Cambridge Live – a Cultural Trust – set up as a charitable company by Cambridge City Council to look after the festival and other live arts and entertainment events in the city and the surrounding area.

THE FOLKIES

The people at Cambridge Folk Festival *love* music. From everything I've heard, read and those I've spoken to, this is an enduring characteristic of the festival – it's a music lover's paradise, for serious and earnest music-lovers. It is perhaps most popular with slightly older generations but also has a lot to offer younger generations and especially aspiring artists and musicians.

The festival is a true centrepiece of the live performance circuit and a lot of people come back year after year and they know where everything is. It's a place to meet new people and see old friends – in fact people plan their year around the event, with punters reuniting year after year at the festival. In fact I remember reading about a young girl saying it was her 16th year in a row at the festival and she was only 16! She had been only two weeks old when she was brought along for the first time. There is something wonderfully exciting about that and it does quash those stuffy and cosy preconceptions of the type of audience that the Cambridge Folk Festival attracts.

Marcus Mumford performs at the Cambridge Folk Festival in 2014.

THE MUSIC

Don't let the word 'folk' put you off. Why should it? Under the banner of 'folk' the festival incorporates so many other genres of music, including jazz, Americana, blues, roots, bluegrass, gospel, Cajun and ceilidhs and various others from all over the world. In fact it's quite hard to be conclusive about defining folk music, probably more so than any other genre. 'Folk music' is defined as an art form that has been passed on from generation to generation, and the festival's open mind results in a tremendous coalescence of sounds and fusions from countless worldwide traditions.

It would be impossible to list or even abbreviate the diversity of artists who have played the festival, but look towards Seasick Steve, Kris Kristofferson, Sinead O'Connor, Van Morrison, Joan Baez, Emmylou Harris, Donovan, The Proclaimers, Jasper Carrot and Billy Connolly as indication as to what is on offer. In fact Connolly was branching out from straight stand-up comedy to folk, but his performance at the festival in 1978 very much transported him back to his roots when he played in The Humblebums. Connolly followed legendary American folk singer/ songwriter Tom Paxton on stage and said it was the best laxative he'd ever known! He then went on to overawe the crowd with his opening track, 'The Shitpickers Waltz'!

KT Tunstall also has an indelible relationship with Cambridge and it was the first festival she ever played following the release of *Eye of the Telescope* in 2004. KT grew up in Fife in Scotland and was part of the successful Fence Collective folk scene in the area along with people like Kenny Anderson (aka King Creosote). Since then she has played the Cambridge Folk Festival on a number of occasions for so many reasons. 'It has a great vibe,' KT recalls, 'and everyone is open to seeing things they have never seen before. It's a great environment for an artist to play a new album as everyone seems in an open-minded state.'

The line-up tries to reflect the many changes in the music scenes over the years and always strives to combine the new and the old. Many established names find it difficult to stay away – in fact it's a regular haunt for Loudon Wainwright III and his children, Martha and Rufus,

> 'THE LINE-UP TRIES TO REFLECT THE MANY CHANGES IN THE MUSIC SCENES OVER THE YEARS AND ALWAYS STRIVES TO COMBINE THE NEW AND THE OLD.'

both of whom have headlined the festival as solo artists. It's a launch pad for many unknown artists too; international acts Mumford & Sons and Noah and the Whale owe Cambridge a debt of gratitude for the support at the start of their careers. One would think that a more 'purist' folk audience such as the one at Cambridge would resent their sharp career trajectory. But not so: diversity and choice is something that is indoctrinated into the history of folk – it's about welcoming and encouraging, not alienating and separating.

The various stages offer a real diversity in talent: Stage One is the big arena, while Stage Two is a more intimate venue; the Club Tent, meanwhile, is hosted by regional folk clubs and also shows off new talent. The Den was specifically set up in 2011 to support emerging talent, and if you fancy getting up and performing yourself then there is the opportunity to book yourself in for a 15-minute slot in the Hub Tent. The idea is to remove the barrier between them and us – the artists and the audience. There are so many opportunities for members of the audience to create their own music all over the site too – in bars, in performance tents, in the campsites, pretty much anywhere on site!

CAMBRIDGE: A PLACE EVERYBODY WANTS TO TELL YOU A STORY!

When asked about Cambridge Folk Festival, I often hear people say they come every year. I want to be included in that conversation and become a regular at the event! Ken Woollard was renowned for his integrity within an industry seldom known for it, and left a legacy behind that continues until this day. Then there's the music: 'These are the songs, tunes and stories of the lands of our fathers – they are part of us,' continues Mark Radcliffe. Folk music means great players, performing great tunes in a really friendly, unpretentious atmosphere with good beer. It is a simple idea of providing the best for artists and audiences alike and the Cambridge Folk Festival is just that – a place everybody wants to tell you a story and there are plenty more stories to be told (although my first stop is going to be the silent Ceilidh!).

Crowds turn out for another Creamfields session in 2000.

DANCE FESTIVALS *Most likely to hear:* A) a whistle.
B) a collection of DJs asking you to scream. C) a collection
of DJs saying 'I can't hear you!' Or all of the above...

Scan here to see Edith's
Dance festivals essentials.

D A

Every festival incorporates dance to a certain degree – most forms of music entice some kind of physical movement, after all. But the dance music scene has seen a surge in popularity in the past few decades, and the growth of dance and electronic music, especially since the illegal rave scene of the late 1980s and early 1990s, has catapulted this once 'niche' genre to the forefront of the festival calendar. Dance music culture infiltrates so many other music genres, and has, of course, sat comfortably alongside other genres at big festivals for decades; but due to the resurgence and the recent marketability of open air dance floors and larger than life raves, this sub-culture has grown into its own unique festival offering, with numerous festivals now catering for dance-heads across the UK.

Before we get into discussing a few of them, the one thing that I always want to know about dance music festivals is this: most of the time DJs are playing other people's music and, come on, let's be honest, how much of it is mixed live? Also, what's the repeat possibility of tunes? I've DJ'd before, and when you hear the DJ before you play what was going to be the second song in your set, it's hugely annoying. Do they submit their set lists before? How do they avoid that?

My dance festival experience stems primarily from my time at MTV where we would travel the length and breadth of the country to film the programme *Dance Floor Chart* from the biggest and best club nights, and dance events. We would normally start filming at midnight and continue throughout the night – just when the fun begins and when you really get to see the heart of the party. We also spent a lot of time in Ibiza and Majorca filming and chatting to 'punters' and DJs. It's a fascinating world, the life of a DJ – particularly that kind of DJ.

'DANCE MUSIC CULTURE INFILTRATES SO MANY OTHER MUSIC GENRES, AND HAS, OF COURSE, SAT COMFORTABLY ALONGSIDE OTHER GENRES AT BIG FESTIVALS FOR DECADES.'

Perhaps the first festival to grow out of the early rave scene and pave the way for other festivals to do the same was Tribal Gathering. Its aim was to bring together the variety of those aforementioned sub-cultures of the dance world under one Dance Music umbrella – from the more mainstream movements such as techno, house and trance, through to the smaller, lesser-known sub-genres such as breakbeat, jungle and the fledgling drum 'n' bass and garage scenes. The festival began in 1993 in Wiltshire with Laurent Garnier, Slipmatt and Pete Tong amongst the DJs taking to the decks to perform in front of approximately 25,000 happy hardcore fans. The 1994 Criminal Justice Bill, however, discouraged outdoor raves, so the festival moved to Munich, Germany for a year, before returning for editions in Oxford in 1995, Bedfordshire in 1996 and a legendary edition in 1997 which saw electronica gurus Kraftwerk headline the festival. Despite its success and the clear market for a dedicated dance music festival, Tribal Gathering eventually fizzled out due to various legal and ownership disputes.

Indeed, the market for this type of event never went away and Tribal Gathering simply provided a platform for other dance festivals to begin to flourish. But what was particularly unique about the scene was its growth via record labels and club nights; with the focus very much on the music and not, necessarily, the performance. Festival promoters were understandably conscious of the market they were catering for and were, at first, hesitant about trying to build a festival on such a broad genre. But with the introduction of dedicated (and popular) club nights and the marketability of cult music labels such as Warp Records, dance music festivals began to flourish and audience numbers began to expand year on year.

As I said in the Introduction to the book, it would be impossible to cover every festival the length and breadth of the country, but what follows is a taster of what our fabulous nation has to offer dance music lovers across the UK. Beginning, of course, with perhaps the most well-known UK (and perhaps internationally-known) dance music festival, Creamfields.

CREAMFIELDS

When I think of dance music festivals I don't automatically think of precious stones, but someone, somewhere once referred to Creamfields as 'The crown jewel of dance festivals.' Apologies for my lack of clarity on the matter but that may simply be down to the sheer number of dance festivals I have frequented... Back to that 'jewel,' it's quite an anachronistic term for what is a largely contemporary music scene, but it also perhaps alludes to the sluggishness of the dance festival scene. Although it's grown over the years, Creamfields is what it always has been – a commercial dance music festival and an event which still has extremely strong ties to its roots. It began in 1998 and grew out of the success of the CREAM night that took place in Liverpool's 'Nation' nightclub in 1992. Established by James Barton, Andy Carroll and Darren Hughes, the club grew very big, very quickly, and an electronic dance music festival seemed to be the natural progression for the event's organisers. A haven for young people to spend their Saturday night listening and dancing to music, CREAM became almost a lifestyle for many clubbers, some of whom travelled from all over the UK to sample the night's irresistible breaks.

The festival's first edition, which took place in 1998, was originally planned as a one-day event and saw around 25,000 people attending the event. Staged in Winchester, the festival was headlined by Primal Scream and Run DMC, and also saw the likes of Sasha, Paul van Dyk and a little-known French dance duo, performing under the moniker 'Daft Punk', take to the decks. It was moved to the countryside location of Daresbury in 2006 – the birthplace of Lewis Caroll, author of *Alice in Wonderland* (there is some kind of irony or a gag opportunity referring to a 'mad hatter's tea party and a field of ravers' but I'm not going to go there!) – where it really began to attract a diverse crowd of dance enthusiasts from across the UK. So much so that the festival was upgraded to a two-day event in 2008 and by 2014 was attracting a massive 70,000 people over the August bank holiday weekend.

Creamfields' success has also allowed its organisers to promote its brand on an international stage, with hugely successful Grammy-nominated album compilation releases and established events taking place in Ibiza, Mallorca, Chile, Brazil, Spain and the Czech Republic. In fact Argentina's edition

'ALTHOUGH IT'S GROWN OVER THE YEARS, CREAMFIELDS IS WHAT IT ALWAYS HAS BEEN – A COMMERCIAL DANCE MUSIC FESTIVAL AND AN EVENT WHICH STILL HAS EXTREMELY STRONG TIES TO ITS ROOTS.'

has become the biggest one-day dance festival in Latin America! Today the brand is managed under the huge 'Live Nation Music' organisation (which also manages Download and the Wireless festivals) – a company that provides a financially stable foundation in what is one of the more turbulent festival markets.

I first attended Creamfields when I hosted the *Dance Floor Chart* on MTV. To me it felt like an extension of club mentality but in the great outdoors, with DJs playing in a few tents in a field with not much else going on. I remember having to perform a 'closing link' to camera whilst pretending to usher cars out of the car park with a high visibility vest on. The weather was atrocious and my producer, who shall remain nameless, wanted a comedy link which included me waving the last car out of the car park, my wellies getting stuck in a puddle and me ending up face down in an enormous muddy puddle that might well have been used for all kinds of dregs! Needless to say it didn't leave me with the most 'tender' connection with the festival!

Unlike those first few years, today Creamfields is massive. With the yearly growth of the festival – in numbers, sites, stages and with the genre having an element of rebirth – the organisers have moved onto a full-blown outdoor festival with two outdoor stages and approximately ten arenas. With size comes expectation, and being able to fill those stages so it's not just about playing the tunes: the visuals and production are important and are taken seriously. It's all about DJs – big name DJs – playing the big tunes, playing them well and to a crowd who know what they have come to hear. It's all about taking the CREAM night into a field for thousands of people who want to have a great night or weekend out, dancing and throwing a few shapes.

Expect lasers, confetti – even a little dry ice! In fact in 2014 there were 16,000 pyro effects, 62 high-powered lasers and 12 miles of streamers. The most commonly used phrases across every stage from the North Stage and South Stage to the All Gone Pete Tong Amp and through Head Kandi hospitality would be: 'Are you ready?' and 'Make some noise!'

As mentioned the line-up is predictably DJ-heavy, with big guns like Calvin Harris, Pete Tong, Paul Okenfold, Sasha, and Fatboy Slim all taking to the Creamfields stage at some point in their glorious careers (I believe that Paul Van Dyk has only missed one Creamfields since it began!). The festival also supports up and coming DJs too – with a number of young, talented DJs dropping their breaks on the hallowed Creamfields decks. Avicii and Skrillex, who opened the North Stage back in 2011, are just a couple of names you might recognise.

Global Gathering, held annually in Stratford Upon Avon, is now one of the premier dance events of the year.

GLOBAL GATHERING

———

Similarly to Creamfields, Global Gathering grew out of the success of an already popular and established club, Code (now 'AIR') – the home of 'Godskitchen', a nightlife institution. With more mainstream clubs expanding to the surrounding fields, it was only a matter of time before the lesser-known clubs began to expand too – with drum n bass, trance and dubstep clubs all exploring opportunities to bring their music to the masses. Godskitchen was one such club: rekindled from the fading embers of the UK rave scene in the early 1990s, the club night began life at the AIR nightclub in Birmingham before expanding south to Milton Keynes and the surrounding areas. Today it is a very successful brand around the world and holds festivals in Russia, Belarus and other countries, entertaining over a million people in 11 different countries. But the jewel in its crown (there's that phrase again) is Global Gathering – one of the most successful and progressive dance music events in the UK

festival calendar. It also has a very young crowd that attracts some great names to play.

Global Gathering started in 2001 and has grown exponentially year on year. Taking place across two long summer days (and nights), the festival houses approximately 85,000 and has twice been voted the 'Best UK Festival' by *DJMag*. Now owned by MAMA & Co (which, along with running some of the country's best loved venues, also operates Lovebox, Wilderness and the Great Escape festivals), Global Gathering isn't necessarily 'family friendly'; its primary aim is to fulfil the needs of its young audience, with some of the edgiest and most impressive electronica performed across its 16 stages.

Global Gathering is held at Long Marston Airfield, the former home of the Phoenix Festival which ran from 1993 till 1998, located just three miles from Stratford-Upon-Avon in Warwickshire, which is incredibly easy to get to by train, car and bus. The site has a splattering of old battered planes that are strewn around the site, which offers a really unique and vivid backdrop to what is a truly visceral festival. This forward-thinking and cutting edge festival is known globally as a 'mecca' of all things dance music and proudly emphasises the underground side of the genre whilst keeping that all-important

commercial appeal.

It started off being purely about the DJs and sound systems from David Morales to Tall Paul to Roni Size and Lisa Lashes. But much in the same way that more traditional festivals have had to evolve with musical cycles to survive, so have dance festivals. Global Gathering quickly developed beyond traditional DJs – until it became about those bands and artists with

'THIS FORWARD-THINKING AND CUTTING EDGE FESTIVAL IS KNOWN GLOBALLY AS A "MECCA" OF ALL THINGS DANCE MUSIC AND PROUDLY EMPHASISES THE UNDERGROUND SIDE OF THE GENRE WHILST KEEPING THAT ALL-IMPORTANT COMMERCIAL APPEAL.'

dance at the heart of their music, such as Daft Punk, Groove Armada, Faithless and Basement Jaxx. Even The Happy Mondays played Global Gathering back in the day!

Dance music legend Paul Okenfold can still pick and choose which festivals he plays and Global Gathering tends to stay at the top of his list. From his experience Global Gathering has always been one

MIA, *who has performed at Global Gathering in previous years.*

of the best gigs to play due to the crowd – an enthusiastic, receptive and impassioned group of people. Tiesto has also been playing for Godskitchen since it started and for him playing festivals is one of the best things to do as a DJ. He also thinks that the presence of dance music at festivals in general has widened the audience for dance music as a whole and Global Gathering has been at the forefront of bringing more esoteric genres to the masses over the years.

The festival is taking a break in 2015, the first since it began, with organisers saying it is to 'allow them to review all elements of the event to ensure it remains at the heart of the UK dance market.' The fans are upset about this, but not as much as locals who benefit from the thousands of pounds raised for charity. There is a huge amount of money donated to local projects and charities through money collected from VIP tickets and discount tickets to residents. I hope it is just a break and time and effort is being put into launching the festival again – it has such a strong following, after all, and is held in high regard not just by those that play it but also those who attend. Quite simply: the audiences at Global Gathering are celebrated for being some of the best on the circuit.

PARKLIFE FESTIVAL

Parklife Festival is an independent music festival, which started life as the 'Mad Ferret Festival'. It began in 2010, so it's quite a young event but one that has quickly grown a massive and loyal following. It's a well-organised festival, put together by the people behind 'The Warehouse' project – a series of Manchester club nights, which took the unique approach of holding events seasonally as opposed to all year round.

Parklife is held in Heaton Park, the biggest municipal park in Manchester and one of the largest parks in Europe. The park itself also has some glorious history: Oasis played three nights to over 200,000 people in 2009 and various theatre productions have been staged there over the years. I've also had past experience of Heaton Park: Radio 1 held one of its Big Weekends there in 2003 and I'd rather not talk about The Stone Roses comeback gigs that took place in Heaton in 2012, as I couldn't make them due to work commitments... (not really bothered about that at all. *Much!*)

Holding the event in Heaton Park – a location that has vital experience of hosting a variety of music events – can only be beneficial for what is essentially a city-based

Below: A bunch of dance-heads turn out for the Parklife Festival in 2014.

Chromeo entertain the main stage at Parklife.

Orlando from The Maccabees.

'THE ORGANISERS MAKE SURE THERE IS MORE MADNESS, MORE MUSIC, MORE DANCING AND MORE FUN THAN YOU WOULD THINK POSSIBLE IN A PARK.'

dance music festival. Being so close to a city centre is, of course, very important too, with travel and accommodation easily accessible. And with Parklife a non-camping festival, the infrastructure of Heaton Park and its close proximity to Manchester city centre is invaluable.

Being in and around a residential area brings its problems for any festival, although they have the full backing of their local council who have said, maybe slightly ambitiously, that they expect the festival to rival Glastonbury! In an attempt to alleviate disgruntled locals, councillors have suggested a surcharge on tickets to allow money from the festival to aid residents living close to the site. Festival organiser Jon Drape says they take the local community very seriously by trying to limit the impact on local areas and he has even brought in a sports ground recovery company to restore the park after the festival. The main issues, of course, with every festival in a city centre are ones of sound and time: it's never going to be loud enough or go on late enough, but those are the concessions the organisers make to enable it to be so close to the city (it's the same issue with Reading and events held in Hyde Park in London). There is, however, nothing wrong with starting the party earlier or heading into town to continue at one of the various venues hosting official after-show parties!

Parklife has a diverse line-up of drum and bass, dubstep, tech, house and a band or two thrown in for good measure, and the organisers make sure there is more madness, more music, more dancing and more fun than you would think possible in a park! It also has a pretty mainstream line-up, with a real emphasis on dance and electro, while also mixing up its DJs, MCs, and bands with the odd theatre and interactive performances.

Snoop Dogg, Foals, Soul II Soul and Gorgon City played the 2014 edition of the festival, whilst previously Dizzee Rascal, Johnny Marr, Disclosure, The Maccabees, Four Tet, Steve Mason and Jurassic 5 have been amongst the names playing in the six performance tents and main stage. Everyone that I've spoken to who has been or played at Parklife talk about its amazing party atmosphere. It just gets better and better and bigger and bigger, and according to my friend Becci Abbot, who manages a number of DJs, 'the new Temple Stage is up there as one of the best UK dance stages at festivals and probably one of the most important festivals now for a DJ.' Thomas Coxhead, who runs *The House Of Coxhead*, one of the most influential dance blogs on the internet, provides the final word: 'after Glastonbury, it's the best festival in the UK.'

![GREEN MAN]

WHERE: *Brecon Beacons, Wales* **WHEN:** *The weekend before the August Bank Holiday*

GREEN MAN
Most likely to see:
A game of cricket next to the Mountain Stage.

SCAN HERE

Scan here to see Edith's Green Man essentials.

The Green Man festival is one of a kind. It is a seven-day event culminating in a bespoke weekend of bands, debates, theatre, science and art that passionately supports local businesses, with a non-corporate ethos and a truly ethical mind. The festival is the largest contemporary music and arts festival in Wales, with a real emphasis on family and community spirit. Many say the setting, Glanusk Park nestled under Sugar Loaf Mountain in the Brecon Beacons National Park in Wales, is one of the most beautiful settings in the UK. Whatever the opinion, the Green Man is a true one-off in the festival calendar and a festival you simply need to attend if you're interested in music, performance or indeed life in general!

THE HISTORY OF THE GREEN MAN

Before I get into the history of the Green Man Festival it is necessary to give you a bit of background on the Green Man himself – who he is and why he's the inspiration for this festival. The Green Man pops up all over the world in various formations, depending on the culture he is residing in and in what time: he could be interpreted as a symbol of rebirth, representing the cycle of growth with leaves, branches or vines protruding from his nose, mouth, nostrils or other parts of the face. Or he could be carved into the dead part of a living oak tree, part plant, part human. Some say he is the Pagan personification of the folk movement. Or perhaps he is a demi-mythological god of the land, with powers to cleanse the soul of the earth during a time of environmental crisis. Ok, that might be taking it a step too far, but the way things are going we are going to need his help in the future! Whatever he is or whatever he represents, each year the festival closes with the spectacular sight of the burning of the Green Man on the Sunday night followed by a few fireworks.

The Green Man Festival has been running since 2003 when it opened as a one-day event for just 300 people. The site is surrounded by the Black Mountains, a range that

The wonderful Daughter perform on the main stage in 2014.

sweeps across the English–Welsh border into Herefordshire and the most eastern range that makes up the Brecon Beacons National Park. Expectations are already high as you approach the festival site, as Will Cook from *The 405* music blog explains: 'The landscape is breathtaking, it kind of sets you up for the whole weekend, you get a sense of leaving it all behind, of anticipation. I'm sure they do it on purpose, that tiny windy road that meanders up into the hills. The road seems to go a bit out of the way – it's a wise move if it is

intentional.' The area of the festival is also arranged over more ley lines than any other festival site in the UK. Sitting amidst ancient oak trees, this naturally creates chemistry with the environment and a relationship between the energy of the land and the people.

The festival was originally founded and started by well-known 'folktronica' duo Daniel and Josephine Hagan and supported by Kenneth Lower. The former duo began the festival on a whim, having moved from London to Brecon at the turn of the century. In 2005

Below: The Black Mountains play host to the Green Man Festival every August.

'THE GREEN MAN FESTIVAL IS THE LARGEST CONTEMPORARY MUSIC AND ARTS FESTIVAL IN WALES.'

Fiona Stewart became managing director of the festival and a few years later became the owner. Today she runs the festival with her son Ben Coleman who books the bands. It's always been a family-run festival with an aim to encourage the audience to embrace the opportunity to escape from everyday life. And what a location to escape to! Fiona Stewart wanted to offer a truly unique event where your mind is opened to different arts and ideas, and with enough content for you to create whatever kind of festival you want.

GREEN MAN TODAY

Fiona Stewart has a wealth of knowledge and experience to draw on having worked at Glastonbury and the Big Chill. The first thing to deal with when she came on board was the location: Glanusk Park is one of the biggest selling points of the festival and Fiona took it upon herself to develop and prepare the site whilst also maintaining its natural beauty. Glanusk Park has an amazing natural landscape, but part of it was a little like someone's back garden and needed a great deal of work to turn it from an agricultural farm into an event site. The hard work has paid off, however, and the site is now pristine and the perfect backdrop for what the festival strives to achieve. It's not about being exclusive but inclusive for one and all. And to maintain that it was important to cap the size of the festival – for it to remain a medium-sized event with the ability for people to wander around and feel comfortable within the setting.

The festival lives and survives in the spirit of collaboration between Fiona and her team who put all their creative energy and expertise into making each corner of the festival unique and carefully crafted. Although a relatively new festival, it feels very grounded and connected. It's incredible that they have managed to maintain no corporate involvement, making the festival a very unique experience but one that is important to the traditional festival organisers. I use the term 'traditional organisers' because Fiona sees the festival as a powerful tool that allows not only creative freedom and expression but also comes with an important message. Avoiding the commercial

'ALTHOUGH A RELATIVELY NEW FESTIVAL, IT FEELS VERY GROUNDED AND CONNECTED.'

investment, however, does bring with it an incredible financial challenge.

The festival has enduring connections and very strong charitable partnerships with Oxfam Cymru, RSPB Cymru, Brecon Beacons National Park Authority and the Bevan Foundation, which is the only charity in Wales committed to tackling all aspects of poverty, inequality and injustice. They also run training programs with Merthyr Tydfil College and the Salvation Army in Cardiff to mentor young vulnerable adults.

Showcasing Welsh talent is another important part of the festival, not just in music but also across the arts. They do a lot of training and development programmes, engaging with various science and arts projects. The organisers have also set up a charitable arm of the festival to operate the non-commercial projects.

Festival goers also get the opportunity to maximise their time in Wales. You can opt for a 'Settlers Pass', which allows you to arrive at the festival nearly a week before it kicks off on the Thursday evening – turning a long weekend into a proper summer holiday! You can experience local attractions and eating in the local area whilst also enjoying many of the events put on specifically for the 'Settlement' area, including their own stage which programmes local Welsh artists.

The site has also been fully waterproofed – demonstrating once again the organisers' commitment to making the festival the premier Welsh, and perhaps British music festival of the year. I'm not entirely sure what 'waterproofing' means, but in my head I have the idea of a giant umbrella engulfing the site – a little far-fetched, I know, but I'm assured it will make a huge difference should the weather god (perhaps that's the Green Man?) look down unfavourably on the site in the future.

The natural amphitheatre that is the Mountain Stage has seen the likes of Van Morrison, Bon Iver, Laura Marling and the Robert Plant rock the Welsh valleys against the phenomenal backdrop of the Black Mountains.

'THE FOOD ON OFFER AT THE FESTIVAL IS GARNERING A GREAT REPUTATION AND IS VERY MUCH ANOTHER BIG ATTRACTION TO GLANUSK PARK.'

Other areas include: The Far Out Fields, which offers late night DJs, film screenings and a real mix of music; and Einstein's Garden, which offers a real fusion of art, science and nature through comedy, music, theatre, walks, talks and interactive workshops. Babbling Tongues, a spoken word area, and Last Laugh, a comedy area, are both new additions to the festival, the latter of which Fiona is keen to develop as a mini-festival in its own right – a festival within a festival! Indeed the

Green Man Beer Festival already runs throughout the weekend, so if you like to get geeky about your beer and cider, then you'll have the perfect opportunity with 99 different local ales and ciders on offer.

But what of the food? The food side of the festival is garnering a great reputation and is very much another big attraction to the festival. Even for the artists! Patti Smith was seen eating at the rotisserie chicken stall in the Walled Garden of the festival in 2013 and gave it her seal of approval from the stage later in the evening. That's the kind of publicity you can only wish for! In fact it's a bit of a regular thing hearing bands and artists either enthuse about the food or make plans during their set on where they might eat later on that day. So be prepared to bump into the odd musician whilst queuing for something delicious. It would seem that every corner of the culinary world is represented at Green Man, whether that be locally sourced ingredients or Caribbean curry, southern street food, North African and Arabic Souk dishes, Mexican, Italian or how about something from the Welsh Venison Centre? It's a far cry from Thai green curry or a hot dog finished off with a doughnut!

Above: The War on Drugs rock the Mountain Stage at the 2014 edition.

WHO ATTENDS GREEN MAN?

—

Above: Babbling Tongues, a spoken word area, and Last Laugh, a comedy area, are both new additions to the festival.

Fiona Stewart is very much from the Michael Eavis school of thought. She seems to subscribe to the idea that attending a festival is a clear way of removing yourself from modern societal constructs. The aim for Green Man is to offer that escape – to leave your worries, your concerns, your objections, your everyday routine at the gates. But more than that, you can strive to have a very personal, fervent connection, possibly even spiritual. Fiona appreciates it's a slightly romantic notion though and agrees 'it's difficult to retain this [outlook] when festivals have become far more mainstream.' People want different experiences from a festival, not everyone wants that spiritual, life-cleansing experience.

Green Man also has a specific area for teens, known as 'SOMEWHERE' – an idea which originated from Fiona's own experience of taking Ben to festivals she was working at. Yes, there are kids' areas at festivals up and down the country, and some brilliant ones at that; you also have kid-friendly festivals, but no one is really catering for the particular, important and explorative teen age group. Young adults of that age are always on the cusp of discovery and not just about music (although at that age I found my musical taste was incredibly personal and something I would either like to keep to myself or perhaps occasionally share). So Green Man has incorporated film-making, art, writing, drama, and fashion projects, as well as free running and sock wrestling into the programme for the 'SOMEWHERE' area. Having taken my youngest to festivals since he was two years old, I can relate to this; he's now six and he gets enough stimulation from just wandering around and being inquisitive about the sights and sounds he sees and humours me by allowing me to drag him into tents to watch bands and artists he has never heard of. I appreciate there is going to come a time when he will tire of that and require some independence. I can't wait until he introduces me to the music, film and other art forms he loves!

The notion of providing something specific for all ages should really give you some indication of the atmosphere of the Green Man festival and the frame of mind of many of those who attend as well as those who run it. It's a festival made by people of all ages, for people of all ages. I've heard a number of friends and colleagues say that it's like being welcomed into Fiona's family and I love to be part of that.

FOLKEY-DOKEY – THE MUSIC OF GREEN MAN

One of my favourite jobs is working at BBC 6Music – it's just the best jukebox in the world! I am constantly inspired and bewildered by the depth and variety of its playlist. Green Man is perhaps the closest festival to the 6Music oeuvre, with artists such as Mogwai, Patti Smith, Sharon Van Etten, Midlake, Local Natives, Phosphorescent, Jon Hopkins, King Creosote, Adam Buxton, Super Furry Animals, and The National all making appearances over the years. I could go on and list at least another 100 of my favourite bands, all of which have played the festival in the short space of time since it started. Patti Smith played there in 2013 – she's top of my list of heroes I am desperate to see live! Apparently when James Blake played the main stage, the bass was so profuse, it was like the sound of a dinosaur coming over the mountain!

With such a huge selection of entertainment over more than ten stages it does mean that you have to make choices as a music fan – you can't see everything, after all – and you need to be prepared as there are going to be clashes. But this is something that Ben Coleman, the curator, really tries to consider when he is putting together the programme. 'I think people need their running shoes at times. There should be 20 minutes where you can catch the two bands you really want to see that are performing around the same time.'

'WITH SUCH A HUGE SELECTION OF ENTERTAINMENT OVER MORE THAN 10 STAGES IT DOES MEAN THAT YOU HAVE TO MAKE CHOICES AS A MUSIC FAN.'

What's great is that the organisers pay attention to music outside of what is being promoted by radio and other media around the UK; they look outside the box for line-up opportunities, not settling for the obvious and what you see on every other festival line-up. Swedish band First Aid Kit, for example, the sisters who I first saw at a club night put on by record company 'Play It Again Sam' in Paris, appeared at the festival in 2010. It wasn't until 2012, when the band released *The Lion's Roar*, that they started getting attention in the UK, despite making their debut appearance some four years before in front of the Black Mountains in Glanusk Park. Green Man is definitely at the forefront when it comes to scheduling bands and artists they believe are going on to bigger and better things.

Other bands have followed similar paths. Mumford & Sons played early doors on the second stage in 2008 and five years later they headlined the Pyramid Stage at Glastonbury. That kind of progression is something that is very healthy for the festival industry as a whole and the music industry – to support new bands coming through. Alt J and Ben Howard are other names that were seen at Green Man before they were playing enormo-domes and winning copious amounts of awards. Surprisingly Ben Howard specifically asked to come back to play the festival, even when he was in the throws of playing packed out shows like the Pyramid Stage at Glastonbury. Usually when artists get to a certain level it becomes harder to convince them to return to the smaller festivals that helped give them a foot up.

The commitment to those new artists and new talent is shown in

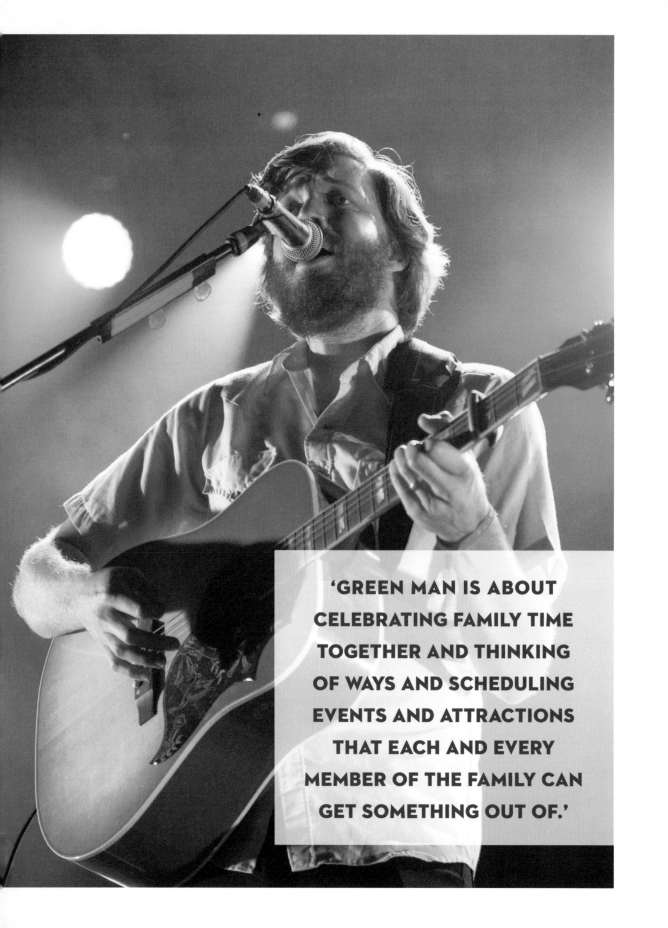

'GREEN MAN IS ABOUT CELEBRATING FAMILY TIME TOGETHER AND THINKING OF WAYS AND SCHEDULING EVENTS AND ATTRACTIONS THAT EACH AND EVERY MEMBER OF THE FAMILY CAN GET SOMETHING OUT OF.'

Left: The amazing Midlake perform at Green Man Festival in 2014.

an online competition run by the festival called Green Man Rising – a competition which is not just about winning a spot to play at the festival but also about offering advice and workshops to help those musicians and individuals understand the business and industry more concisely. The Rising Stage is for emerging talent with the added bonus of offering mentoring in stage direction and technical support. Having a greater understanding of how to promote yourself or making sure you get the best out of your performance through the right sound and production techniques is something that is unique to Green Man and a fantastic source of support and advice.

A FESTIVAL FOR ALL GENERATIONS

—

The symbolism of the Green Man mirrors so much of what the festival aims to achieve. The messages and wishes that are written and placed inside the Green Man at the festival are touching and show a real belief in something greater. This idyllic and perhaps even old fashioned notion of sitting around the bonfire as if you were in a film, chatting away to a variety of friends and family from a variety of generations but with a common point of reference – is at the very heart of the Green Man Festival. Will Cook said that he 'always scoffed at people when they said that a festival was an essential part of their summer, mainly because I don't think it's healthy to repeat yourself too much. Somehow Green Man has become that thing I need each summer – to recharge and centre myself for the rest of the year.' From talking to so many people about Green Man, the thing that makes it stand out is that it's not just about being a family festival, it's about celebrating family time together and thinking of ways and scheduling events and attractions that each and every member of the family can get something out of.

Blonde-bombshell Simon from Biffy Clyro tunes up on the main stage at Reading. Why so serious?

READING AND LEEDS

WHERE: *Reading and Leeds* **WHEN:** *August Bank Holiday*

READING AND LEEDS

Most likely to see: A teen celebrating/weeping over their
GCSE results while singing along to 'Basket Case'.

Scan here to see Edith's
Reading and Leeds essentials.

The Reading Festival is the world's oldest and most enduring popular music festival. Ask any band around the world and they will know about the Reading Festival, and can probably name you at least a handful of performances from over the years. I use the word 'legendary' very rarely, but I think Reading has more than earned that reputation for being about the music first and foremost. From my point of view bands reap the rewards by showing commitment to Reading and Leeds and putting the work in. I don't just mean in terms of billing and financially, I mean creatively bands are encouraged to do things their way and to try to make it special for the Reading and Leeds crowd. The location is pretty unique too: it's relatively small and compact, and there aren't many festivals where you can get off the train and

The crowd gather for the evening headliner at the 2014 edition of the Reading festival.

be on site in ten minutes' walk. That, of course, has its downsides: you may be only ten or so minutes' walk from the performance arenas but its close proximity to the city centre means there are certain sound restrictions and the festival can't be as loud as it should be. I've been to both the Reading and Leeds sites and there is an obvious difference to how loud the main stage is. It is not a problem in the music tents, but on the main stage it has been known to aggravate bands and fans alike. This is only a small matter that clearly doesn't affect the continued success of the festival. I feel a bit spoilt that I can jump on a train every summer and be at such a legendary event and in the presence of the world's most exciting and successful bands!

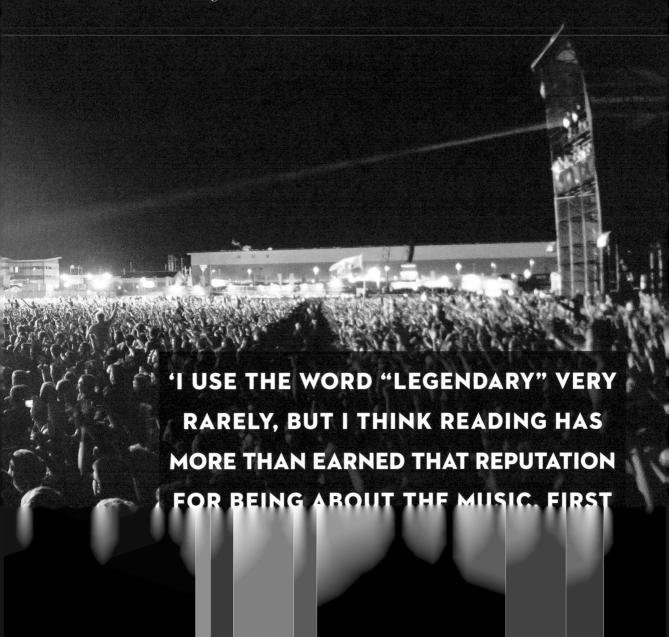

'I USE THE WORD "LEGENDARY" VERY RARELY, BUT I THINK READING HAS MORE THAN EARNED THAT REPUTATION FOR BEING ABOUT THE MUSIC, FIRST

TWO CITIES UNITED IN MUSIC

Reading Festival has the National Jazz Festival to thank for its existence. Harold Pendleton, founder of the Marquee Club, one of the most important music venues in London and possibly Europe (which shaped the music culture of the capital by supporting some of the most seminal bands and artists of all time, from Jimi Hendrix to Joy Division, David Bowie to The Clash), also established The National Jazz Festival in 1961, originally held at Richmond Athletic Ground. By 1964 the name also incorporated 'Blues' into its title, reflecting the change in the music scene with bands such as Cream and Fleetwood Mac playing at the retitled National Jazz and Blues Festival. It was an event that connected with people, and by 1971 was not only attracting crowds of around 30,000 people but moved permanently to a new base in Reading. Over the next few years the numbers grew to 70,000 people,

and with the name change in 1976 to 'Reading Rock', the transformation and beginning of the legendary Reading Festival had begun.

The festival has had a few official titles in relation to sponsors over the years but has always been affectionately known as the 'Reading and Leeds' festival. The modern guise of the festival has always catered for a rock crowd – from progressive rock and blues, to hard rock, punk rock, and new wave. Occasionally this has led to a clash of fans, but nothing sinister or lengthy. In fact, the intertwining of music genres throughout the decades has pushed the festival to its absolute limit: in 1984 and 1985 the council banned the festival by reclaiming the land and refusing a licence, even though a number of acts were already booked and tickets had gone on sale. In 1986 permission was granted for fields close to the original festival site to open for camping and the following year not only saw the biggest audience ever, but was also regarded the last of the 'classic' rock years (although I would argue that 'classic' rock never dies!).

The late 1980s and 1990s saw a change in management, with Harold Pendleton leaving as the head organiser of the festival. The subsequent years followed a goth and indie music policy, bringing with it a drop in numbers as the hair metal gods dominated the line-up. By 1988 the festival was declared bankrupt and organisers were forced to tout 50 per cent of the festival to a number of music and festival promoters across the UK. The majority said 'no', except Vince Power, who at the time was running The Mean Fiddler group, and Melvin Benn, who at the time was running the Workers Beer Company and had been organising

> ## 'THERE IS A SIGNIFICANT DIFFERENCE BETWEEN THE TWO SITES: READING IS CONSIDERED A NATIONAL FESTIVAL AND LEEDS IS CONSIDERED A NORTHERN FESTIVAL.'

free festivals for years. Power and Benn saved the festival over the next few years and were one of the main reasons the festival transformed into the behemoth loved by many today.

The festival's reinvention naturally lead to a greater demand for attendance and the original location in Reading just couldn't cope – the site, after all, was pretty fixed in terms of the size due to its location in the city centre. The ambitious and progressive organisers thus decided to split the festival in two and the Leeds arm was born in 1999. Since then the sites have run simultaneously over the August bank holiday weekend, with mirrored line-ups playing over both sites. But there is a significant difference between the two sites: Reading is considered a national festival and Leeds is considered a northern festival. The former is a national festival because it's been there forever and has a huge amount of history. Conversely, Leeds has a wonderfully grateful northern feel to it, particularly from a music point of view. 'When I get to Leeds I feel more at home,' remarks festival organiser and proud Yorkshireman Melvin Benn. 'People talk to you more and banter with you, sit and pass the time of day with you more. It's the north – people feel appreciative.'

I completely agree: as mentioned, a lot of London audiences have an indifference to them, not through any forced arrogance but simply by being spoilt rotten for choice. I've been on the road with my husband and his band Editors a fair few times and you do find yourself comparing crowds from venue to venue, city to city, festival to festival. And at times a London crowd can be significantly more subdued than other parts of the country.

'READING IS NOT
JUST ABOUT MULTI-
STAGE ROCK BUT
MULTI-GENRE MUSIC
AND PERFORMANCE.'

THE TWO FESTIVALS TODAY

Today both festivals have a huge number of stages offering an incredible array of genres within a very loose framework of 'rock music.' Held every year over the August bank holiday weekend, the Reading site is located at Little John's Farm in central Reading while Leeds, although originally held at Temple Newsam in its eponymous city, moved to Bramham Park, the grounds of a historic house near Wetherby, in 2003.

I think the success and survival of Reading is down to the organisers having a very open mind to what the festival should be offering music-wise. As mentioned, the changing music scene has caused the festival numerous problems and issues to work through, notably to do with its identity. During the late 1980s and early 1990s, for example, the illegal rave scene was developing, appealing to a group of people who couldn't be further away from Reading Festival. With a new team in place, however, the organisers embraced these new trends and continued to research scenes going on in other parts of the world that they felt would help maintain and support their own festivals. Melvin Benn, for example, remembers being in Munich and paying attention to the rave scene out there in an early incarnation of Tribal Gathering – a scene that was not only huge in Germany and other parts of Europe but a great example of how successful an event could be when focused on listening to music and partying in a non-conventional space. It was about taking that ethos and applying it to Reading festival, and appreciating it's not just about multi-stage rock but multi-genre music and performance.

Left: Biffy Clyro rocks the main stage at Reading.

A POST-EXAM-RESULT PARTY!

The Reading and Leeds festivals have a unique selling point for one particular section of the audience: they take place just after the release of exam results and thus have a real connection with teenagers at a time when they are about to embark on a new chapter and make decisions that could potentially shape the rest of their lives – a scary prospect for any 16 or 17 year old! Thinking back, I had no idea what I wanted to do when I was 16, but if I'd had the Reading and Leeds festivals as an opportunity to let off steam, to release tension and make some self-discoveries, I would have jumped at the chance! The combination of unleashed energy in a site full of unbridled opportunities and fun sends the vibrancy off the scale; you really feel that energy on the site – there's a real lust for life (to quote Iggy Pop!).

I know so many friends and bands themselves who did just that!

Will Champion from Coldplay, who attended Reading in 1994, remembers calling home from a phone box to get his GCSE results before heading into the festival. Once inside, he missed Jeff Buckley by ten minutes after he followed his friends, who were all into acid jazz and wanted to watch Jamiroquai. He recalls 'having fun, ambling around, and hearing a whisper on the breeze that would entice you into a tent to listen to something…'

Will's first Reading experience, however, began with a slightly more anxious feeling. After arranging to meet a friend from Cardiff at Reading bus station, Will waited a further two hours for his mate to turn up. Unfortunately for Will, the friend didn't turn up, and at that time he didn't have a mobile phone so had no way of contacting him. He did have his ticket, however, and decided to head in. By the time he made it through security it was beginning to get dark and not only had he never seen that many people in one place, but he'd never been to a festival before and had no idea of where anything was. With his rucksack and tent on his back he headed to the gates and had a romantic notion that he would just casually bump into his mate who would be waiting for him by the corner of the festival, completely unaware of the enormity of the event. After a while of wandering around with a mixture of awe and panic, he found a fence post and sat down. A few hours later he was close to giving up and was about to head to the aforementioned phone box when a familiar face walked past. It turned out to be someone he'd met in a pub in Southampton a few weeks earlier, and elated to see someone he knew and someone who knew where and how to pitch his tent, things began to look up. The next day Will decided to head to the main meeting point, thinking that his Cardiff mate would have the same thought. Guess what? He did!

It is an easy festival to attend and so it really appeals to people who don't want to have to make any more of an effort than to pitch a tent and watch music with their mates.

Below: Foals' Yannis says 'hi' to the Reading faithful.

THE MUSIC

Music is the main exponent of the Reading and Leeds festivals. In fact there's very little else going on – apart from the comedy and performing arts tents. This is something Melvin Benn, the managing director of Festival Republic which runs the Reading and Leeds festivals, is all too aware of: 'People always say to me, what's your favourite festival? Reading will always be my favourite, not just because it was the first, not just because of the success, but also because of its position in society, because of its purity and it's still all about the music. It's incredibly optimistic; it's about being at that point in your life and looking forward. Everybody there is young, it's not an age thing – it's a state of mind, and that results in a particular atmosphere and outlook. I first experienced the festival back in 1972. It had only been running for two years but it made a lasting impression on my mate and me. We hitchhiked down from Yorkshire to spend the weekend at the festival when we were just 16. I didn't know what it was – my friend asked me and we just left – no bags, no tent but we had a great time. We crawled under the main stage and slept under there. Then on the Monday hitchhiked back to Yorkshire, which wasn't easy as on the bank holiday in 1972 there weren't that many cars and particularly lorry drivers on the road to get home.'

Reading has played host to some iconic and legendary performances, not least having Nirvana play twice, one of which included the memorable arrival of Kurt Cobain in a wheelchair in 1992. It was a truly seminal Reading set and for me sums up what the festival has always strived to stand for: authenticity, powerful and creative performances and fun.

Other bands also exemplify the Reading and Leeds ethos: when Rage Against the Machine headlined back in 1996 they came on stage and announced, 'we are Rage Against the Machine, from Los Angeles, California,' before playing the most blistering set many had and will ever see. Hundreds of bodies were flying over the barriers while thousands of music fans were united in their love of the music. Four years later – and only six weeks before their initial split in 2000 – Rage Against

The Machine left the crowd on their knees again (and came back to do the same in 2008).

There is a want and need to headline the Reading and Leeds festival for a certain group of bands; it's something many strive to achieve, it's a point to aim for and many bands see it as a high watermark of their careers. I heard a tale that prior to their world-domination phase (circa 1994,) Oasis were approached to fill the pre-headliner slot that was

'READING HAS PLAYED HOST TO SOME ICONIC AND LEGENDARY PERFORMANCES, NOT LEAST HAVING NIRVANA PLAY TWICE, ONE OF WHICH INCLUDED THE MEMORABLE ARRIVAL OF KURT COBAIN IN A WHEELCHAIR IN 1992.'

vacant as another band had pulled out. Noel Gallagher responded by saying they would love to be on the bill but they wouldn't play before anyone else, that they wanted to headline. It was a great indication of the confidence the band had in their music and their fans, but also a great show of faith from the festival in a band who were really just starting out, but were capable of rising to the occasion.

The idea of supporting bands and showing belief has been around for years and a lot of festivals have a similar ethos. It's something that Reading and Leeds have been doing from the start – backing those bands that were 'rocklings', such as Arctic Monkeys in 2005 packing out what was the then Carling Tent (now the Festival Republic Stage,) in the early afternoon. A similar thing happened to Queens Of The Stone Age and Spiritualized on the Melody Maker Stage in 1998 and Aphex Twin headlining the 3rd Stage in 2002; they were all relatively niche bands that suddenly broke through the mainstream based on one amazing performance. The same thing happened to Radiohead, who played a mid-afternoon set in 1994 before *The Bends* was released, and then went on to headline the festival in 2009. Matt Bellamy from Muse said it would only confirm to him that his band had made it when they headlined the Reading Festival and they did so in 2006 and also in 2011. That particular headline show was one of my favourites: such a unique and creative way to approach an important show, by performing the whole of *Origin of Symmetry*, complete with matching production to the art work of the 2001 album sleeve.

Foo Fighters played their first ever UK performance at the festival before they had even released an album or a single. They didn't just appear in a random slot in the middle of the day – they headlined the NME/Radio 1 Stage. This was in the pre-internet days, so there was no way of being able to download or listen and learn the songs ahead of the appearance. It was all down to Dave Grohl and the history Nirvana had with the festival. The organisers and the band were under an incredible amount of pressure from *NME* magazine to play the main stage, but neither Dave Grohl nor the organisers wanted them to play the main stage. Melvin Benn spent most of the show passing messages to Dave Grohl to get him to calm the crowd down.

READING, LEEDS AND ME

I first went to Reading after moving to London many moons ago and my first Reading experience was with MTV. I was supposed to be hosting with two fellow VJs (video jockey), but the two of them had definitely got far too into the rock'n'roll sprit of the festival by indulging in the fruits of Mr J Daniels' 'flavour-some juice' whereas I, on the other hand, at least managed to do the work. Someone had to! Thus, on the final day it was down to Bowman to fly solo and interview everyone, from DJ Touche to Garbage, and Roni Size to Shed Seven!

Since I have worked at so many of the festivals over the years it's always hard to immerse in the full experience and I never get to see as much as I would like to. What it has allowed me to do over the years, or encouraged me to do, is get on site early and dart around the various stages to listen to as much as possible. One band I was lucky enough to see at Reading was Foals in 2008 and again in 2010 in the NME/Radio 1 Tent. Their performance of 'Spanish Sahara' in 2010, with the entire audience instructed to sit down inside the tent by the band, moved me to tears, and is a perfect example of how a band is perfectly in tune with its audience. They're a band that never holds back and throws themselves, almost physically, into their performance. In fact I might have even witnessed guitarist Jimmy Smith motion to a roadie to place a bucket behind his amp into which he vommited mid-song. The only time I've been that emotional was watching the last ever peformance from Sam Herlihy's Hope of The States in 2006. That and Daphne and Celeste being bottled off stage in 2000!

Right: Festivalgoers rock out in front of the main stage at Reading.

TWO CLASSIC FESTIVALS

—

Scan here to listen to Will Champion's festival memories.

Reading is one step ahead of so many festivals: it has the history, the heritage with music and it has survived for so many years where others have fallen by the wayside. That is down to its musical integrity: by booking the best bands and supporting new and exciting talents, but also looking to the future and among its contemporaries to allow itself to welcome new genres into its world.

Reading is not narrow-minded about music and isn't ageist or judgemental; the festival is about encouraging creativity and being a platform to have fun and enjoy yourself – particularly for a younger audience who are letting go for the very first time. Remember what that feels like and take that feeling with you onto the site. You will have the most exhilarating experience ever.

FESTIVAL NO.

WHERE: *Portmeirion, Wales* **WHEN:** *Penultimate weekend of August*

FESTIVAL NO.6
Most likely to see:
Beck on a golf buggy.

Scan here to see Edith's
No.6 essentials.

Festivalgoers enjoy the sumptuous surroundings of Portmeirion and the wonderful Festival No.6.

Set on its own private peninsular on the southern shores of Snowdonia overlooking Cardigan Bay, nothing can properly prepare you for the first time you experience Festival No.6 and the surrounding landscape and setting. Breathtaking, beautiful, curious, colourful, it really confuses your senses. The journey there alone, and it's a pretty long one, allows you the luxury of experiencing some of the country's most dramatic sights before you are engulfed in subtropical woodlands on one side and miles of sandy beach on the other.

I'd heard friends and colleagues regularly raise the subject of Festival No.6 over the last few years, recounting their genuine fondness of the setting, the atmosphere and the line-up. It was beginning to bother me slightly that I'd not had the opportunity to visit the festival, for whatever reason. Never one to miss out on anything that my contemporaries rave about, especially when it comes to music festivals, I made it my mission to attend with haste. The Portmeirion-based festival has only been running for a few years, but it already has every creative head I know eager to partake in the celebration of music and the arts, in what is an incomparable, offbeat and altogether unique location.

THE HISTORY

'THE FESTIVAL WAS STARTED WITH THE AIM OF THROWING THE TYPE OF PARTY THE ORGANISERS WOULD LIKE TO ATTEND.'

Festival No.6 began back in 2012 and takes place on either the first or second weekend in September. Its host, the village of Portmeirion, was built between 1925 and 1975 by English born Welsh architect Sir Clough Williams-Ellis who claims direct descent from Owain Gwynedd, Prince of North Wales, and who is also the grandfather of Welsh novelist Robin Llewellyn.

Built into a rock face above the estuary of the River Dwyryd, the village was designed in the style of an Italian village and pays tribute to the atmosphere of the Mediterranean, in particular to Williams-Ellis' love of the Italian town of Portofino. Indeed Portmeirion provided the architect with a great deal of pleasure in his lifetime: it was a project that he worked on for many years and a place he adored and spent time in well into his older years. His motto was 'Cherish the past, adorn the present, construct the future' – a philosophy that could easily be translated into what the festival stands for today.

The town has historically been influential and inspirational for many writers and other visionaries, including Noël Coward who wrote the wonderful and critically acclaimed play *Blithe Spirit,* whilst staying in the village. It was also the inspiration behind 1960s spy drama *The Prisoner,* which tells the story of a former British spy held prisoner in a mysterious coastal village. Starring Patrick McGoohan, the drama was a hit with a post-Cold War television audience and helped put Portmeirion on the map after the exteriors for the show were filmed in the village (although this isn't disclosed, as requested by Sir Clough Williams-Ellis, until the opening credits of the last episode of the series). The main character in the drama is referred to as either 'The Prisoner' or 'Number six' and his character – a 'free-thinking, individual forever questioning the staus quo' (according to Festival No.6's website) – is the main inspiration for the name of the festival. It's something the organisers didn't want to geek out on when it came to maintaining an air of *Prisoner* nostalgia with the festival. They were surprised how many bands still love the show, but they also had to keep in mind that there is a large number of audience members who have never heard of it. It's about neither type feeling excluded – that is the key.

The festival was started with the aim of throwing the type of party the organisers – Meurig Jones, Gareth Cooper, Bradley Thompson, Luke Bainbridge and David Exley – would like to attend. At first they thought it would be a once in a lifetime opportunity, but little did they know they were starting something that would give birth to a labyrinthine of music and art for years to come. Luke Bainbridge, a member of the team behind Festival No.6, remembers how the conversation about starting the festival began after Alex Hardee from Coda (an artists' agency that represents bands such as Animal Collective and a few well-known DJs) had been to Mark Jones'

'FESTIVAL NO.6 WAS FOUNDED IN A LOCATION THAT PROVIDED THE MOST ENIGMATIC BLANK CANVAS TO USE AS A SPRINGBOARD TO DELIVER A STRONG ARTISTIC AND CULTURAL ADVENTURE.'

(from the Wall Of Sound record label) wedding in Portmeirion. After a chance meeting with Robin Llewellyn, Luke jokingly suggested they should start a music festival and to his surprise Robin agreed. This was back in 2000 when the festival market was oversaturated and everyone said they were 'crazy, to even entertain the idea'. Meurig, Gareth, Bradley, Luke and David had all been part of the festival scene for 20 years in one way or another, but genuinely felt that nothing was really speaking to their age group or musical tastes. Over those years the average festival audience expectation evolved and you certainly couldn't get away with just putting a few stages up in a field and selling Thai green curry and doughnuts. The 21st century festival audience want and need a fully immersive experience – they want to be tried and tested. Thus Festival No.6 was born, and in a location that provided the most enigmatic blank canvas to use as a springboard to deliver a strong artistic and cultural adventure. Its aim was to provide a unique experience, not just for the audience but for bands and artists too, encouraging them to do something out of the ordinary and different with their performance. That doesn't suit everyone and the organisers take time to search for like-minded artists who are interested in putting on a more left-field experience.

FESTIVAL NO.6 TODAY

East India Youth perform at Portmeirion Town Hall.

It's an incredible achievement for a festival so young to have such unwavering support from artists, while also maintaining a clear purpose to be different and succeed. Festival No.6 is sophisticated without being pretentious, and progressive without being exclusive. As mentioned, the location really is the main draw and sets the scene for what is a truly spectacular festival. The town is a colourful friend that welcomes you with a cluster of creativity while the woodland trails and surrounding area become their own character in your adventure, providing an alternative setting for the numerous bands and artists with their talks, installations, interaction and collaborations.

Tim Burgess and his Tim Peaks Diner has become a regular fixture on the line-up. Curated by Tim and based in the town hall, you feel you have been invited to a creative coffee morning where you can actually sample the fabulous coffee and cake, but also be entertained and enthralled by acoustic gigs, talks, DJ sets and even welsh language classes.

The main arena is based just outside the town in Castell Park, which sits between Portmeirion and Castell Deudraeth on the banks of the River Dwyryd. It's a beautiful location, overlooked by the castle and sweeping fields that lead down towards the woods and town and includes the majority of the main stages: Stage No.6, The iStage, The Clough Stage, the Dance tents, the Late Night Pavilion, Studio 6 and the Castell Gardens (as well as an array of food and beverage outlets, including the particularly impressive Cheese on Toast stall!).

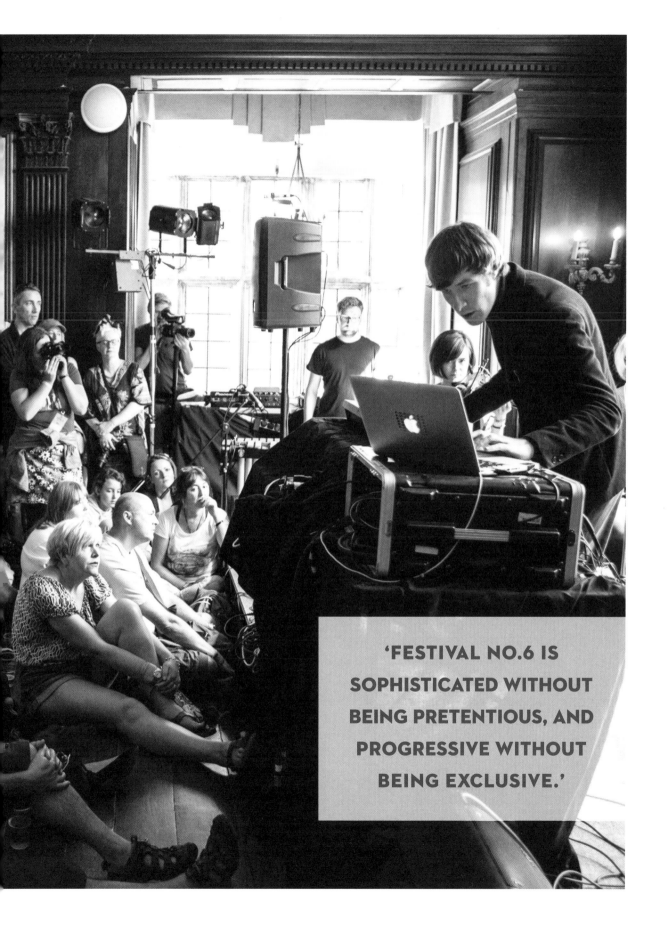

'FESTIVAL NO.6 IS SOPHISTICATED WITHOUT BEING PRETENTIOUS, AND PROGRESSIVE WITHOUT BEING EXCLUSIVE.'

If you're thinking of attending Festival No.6 be prepared for the unexpected. Think of it as a sight-seeing music festival where you might be watching a band one minute, paddle boarding the next or taking part in a torch light procession and then having a ukulele lesson before watching a late-night film.

The sleeping arrangements will fuel your need for an adventure – whether you want to sleep in a castle, a tipi or your own tent. With two distinct sites – the town and the more familiar setting of a festival arena – there's more opportunity to have a different kind of festival experience. In fact it's a bit like being on a seaside holiday with the added benefit of a fantastic festival taking place!

WHO ATTENDS FESTIVAL NO.6?

The organisers of Festival No.6 hold their attendees' interests close to their heart. They're the most important part of the festival, after all – not the sponsors or promoters. They take into consideration issues of identity, which Festival No.6 organiser Luke Bainbridge says 'is a nice thing to play with.' The audience are almost like invited guests of the organisers – everything is aimed at them, the party and festival is all about providing them with the best experience ever (kind of like trying to impress a new boyfriend/girlfriend). Luke wanted to throw a party that he and his mates would want to attend and it has grown, just like a party, through word of mouth. Festival No.6 is an experience that is difficult to put into words: therefore you have to actually go there to see what all the fuss is about. In fact, just being on the train with quite a few journalists was quite surprising: I've never seen such positivity and genuine excitement from such a large group of music journalists and wordsmiths.

The festival's debut year saw approximately 7,000 to 9,000

'THE AUDIENCE ARE ALMOST LIKE INVITED GUESTS OF THE ORGANISERS – EVERYTHING IS AIMED AT THEM, THE PARTY AND FESTIVAL IS ALL ABOUT PROVIDING THEM WITH THE BEST EXPERIENCE EVER.'

people descend upon Portmeirion, with the organisers capping its capacity at 10,000. Now the site has a capacity of 15,000 but that,

*Above: Childhood at
Festival No. 6.*

unfortunately, is the absolute limit. Portmeirion is significantly limited geographically, with no room to expand across any part of the small town; but this allows No.6 to maintain that sense of intimacy, which is such an important part of the festival's character and identity. People feel like they are part of the festival because it is interactive, immersive and, of course, truly intimate.

Beck, a big fan of *The Prisoner*, headlined the festival in 2013, and someone took him round the site on a golf buggy so he could see some familiar sights. The same year Martin Ware from Heaven 17 was behind a 3D music installation and as they were driving around Beck saw him, and jumped off the buggy to have his picture taken with him. Later that evening he professed to the crowd that Festival No.6 was 'the weirdest and most surreal' festival he'd ever been to and asked to play it every year. That type of validation should not be underestimated when it comes to other artists being approached to play the festival or just word of mouth through music fans.

THE MUSIC – 'CHERISH THE PAST, ADORN THE PRESENT, CONSTRUCT THE FUTURE'

It's not just about the music at Festival No.6 and this feeling of creativity is emphasised by the multifaceted transformations of each stage. The main live stage, Stage No.6, embodies the Portmeirion philosophy created by Clough Williams-Ellis, which celebrates the past, present and the future. Pet Shop Boys, Neneh Cherry, Temples, Peter Hook and Beck have all headlined Stage No.6 in the first few years of the festival; London Grammar headlined in 2014 after opening the stage the year before. The London Grammar journey is a great example of the support shown by the festival. The organisers show a lot of faith in raw talent and are not afraid of supporting upcoming bands by offering them their headline slots. London Grammar's headline performance in 2014 was only the third time the band had been given the chance to put on a full headline show anywhere in the world!

The iStage is all about fresh, cutting-edge talent and in a nod to its European festival counterparts, it flip-flops with Stage No.6 so you don't miss a thing, and both stages are never operating at the same time! Jon Hopkins, Steve Mason, Nadine Shah, Denai Moore and East India Youth have all played the iStage over the years, amongst many other cutting-edge talents. Later on in the evening the iStage becomes the Late Night Pavilion, hosting the likes of Julio Bashmore and Laurent Garnier. Studio 6 – also known as the Clough Stage during the daytime – provides the second dance area of the festival. Under its Clough Stage guise it provides a fantastic mix of Welsh and international artists and collaborations.

The Manic Street Preachers, who headlined in 2013, came out of a three-year hiatus to perform at the festival. They said that they wouldn't have come back for anything else. 'So many people had raved about the first year – the setting and the atmosphere, as well as the Welsh male choir performing "Blue Monday",' they said before they played the main stage. In fact, the Manics shot the cover for *This*

'IT'S NOT JUST ABOUT THE MUSIC AT FESTIVAL NO.6 AND THIS FEELING OF CREATIVITY IS EMPHASISED BY THE MULTIFACETED TRANSFORMATIONS OF EACH STAGE.'

Is My Truth down the road from the festival and a lot of the artwork is from around the area. And in a weird twist of fate, the day they played No.6 was almost 15 years to the day that that album was released. That kind of thing really floats my boat!

'THIS IS A FESTIVAL WITH A VERY CLEAR VISION OF WHAT IT IS AND WANTS TO BE.'

Festival No.6's reputation already precedes it. Everything Everything played the first two years of the festival and they were particularly taken with how the festival was never over-crowded or over-policed: 'you can roam and experience places and sites freely and easily,' they said, 'especially as it's quite a small festival.' Jon Hopkins was also desperate to play after his collaborator and No.6 alumni King Creosote told him about the amazing little village and encouraged Jon to play. Other festivals were suggested over that particular weekend, but Jon was adamant that he wanted to do No.6, and do it properly so the weekend was kept clear to allow him to fully experience the festival both as a performer and as a festival fan. Also the chance to play in Wales can be a rarity – there aren't that many festivals or venues to play in for a certain level of artist.

Festival No.6 might also be the only festival to have a composer in residence, replete with eight-piece string ensemble, available at the drop of a hat for artists and performers. Indie-folk band Daughter took full advantage of that luxury in 2013, as did Steve Mason to a packed out Town Hall. Where else would you get that sort of opportunity at a festival, both from the point of view of the artist as well as a festival goer? And don't get me started on the Brythoniaid Welsh Male Voice Choir, which is affectionately referred to as the 'No.6 boy band'. The group of men, aged between 70 and 85, celebrated their 60th anniversary at the festival in 2014.

FESTIVAL NO.6 AND ME

My first experience of Festival No.6 was pretty magical and memorable. I went alone. I find that experience in itself pretty empowering but it also means I can be totally selfish: I have no one to answer to, no one to argue with about who or what we see, and I have more time to explore as opposed to wasting time trying to find other members of my group. It's not ungenerous – it's being self-sufficient! Even the journey down there – a good three hours from central London – was like being on a school trip. Entertainment had been arranged on the train down to Bangor – an ingenious idea to while away the time: spoken word poetry from Mike Garry and Luke Wright, and comedy from Phil Kay was a complete joy to witness on the journey, especially Mike's poem *St Anthony*, his tribute to Anthony H. Wilson, which he later performed at the festival with an orchestra, alongside his touching and powerful poem to his late mother, *What Me Mam Taught Me*. The journey felt like an authentic introduction to what No.6 has to offer. It set the bar not only of the standard of performance but more about the spirit of the festival; it definitely got me in the mood.

Right: Festival goers enjoy a ukulele class.

A WONDERFUL JOURNEY OF MUSIC AND CREATIVITY

This is a festival with a very clear vision of what it is and wants to be. It's not a festival for people who want to hear mainstream or chart music; it's not about the latest fashionable genre or scene; it's for everyone from 18 to 80 who want to go on a wonderful journey of music and creativity, and to encounter some of the freshest and most interesting talents currently plying their trade on the ever-changing music scene.

It's important to appreciate how hard it is to establish a new festival, but with No.6 they seem to have tapped into something that people want to see and hear – a genuine niche in the festival market which caters for the laid-back, open-minded and creative consumer. It's a true accomplishment in what is a very competitive market and I hope we will see this festival endure for many more successful years to come.

Revelers settle back for another glorious day of music at V Festival.

WHERE: *Hylands Park and Weston Park*   **WHEN:** *August Bank Holiday*

V FESTIVAL *Most likely to see:* Denim shorts with colourful socks protruding from the top of wellies and a hair garland of some sort on at least 96.4 per cent of the females in attendance!

Scan here to see Edith's V essentials.

I think people are very quick to judge V Festival, for whatever reason. It's a hugely popular festival that caters for a wide demographic – from indie-junkies to pop-princesses. The name, of course, is twofold: the festival is sponsored by Virgin while the majority of its audience are going to a festival for the very first time. And truthfully, it is a great one to start with. V doesn't test or stretch you on any level – it's a good size, has great facilities and includes some of the best music acts of the year. It's like a starter pack for festivals!

'THE FESTIVAL IS GREGARIOUS, BRASH AND NOT SUBTLE IN ANY WAY WHEN IT COMES TO BRANDING AND ADVERTISING ON THE SITE.'

THE HISTORY OF V

You might be surprised to learn that the idea for the V Festival came about back in 1996 when Jarvis Cocker revealed he wanted to play two different outdoor venues in one day – a kind of north and south musical opportunity. The idea soon grew into having multiple stages with camping available for people to spend the weekend. Two sites were originally suggested – Victoria Park in Warrington and Hylands Park in Chelmsford – but due to the restricted size of Victoria Park, in its first year there was only one day of performances in Warrington and two days at Hylands Park in Chelmsford. Over the next few years the northern leg moved to Temple Newsam in Leeds, which now hosts the Leeds leg of the Reading and Leeds Festival. In 1999, V moved and settled on the site it still uses today, Weston Park in Staffordshire. In the past the name of the festival would change reflecting the particular year – V96, V99 for example – but in 2003 the name was changed to V Festival.

The event is very much one of the more commercial festivals and if you stand still for too long you may well end up with some kind of logo attached to you! Joking aside, with that huge commercial element comes a level of mainstream expectation and interest: the festival is gregarious, brash and not subtle in any way when it comes to branding and

Above: Kasabian rock the main stage at V.

advertising on the site. But if this is your first festival that is the last thing you are going to pay attention to.

Organiser Andy Redhead compares setting the site up in Weston Park to that of erecting a small town and the associated infrastructure that comes with it. They have to bring everything in – the water supply, power, waste disposal, fire station and even a hospital – all run by over 2,500 staff. If you do head to V Festival look out for one particular member of staff – a gentleman who goes by the name of 'Kiss'. His job is 'Head of Power'! What a title. He is positioned underneath the main stage for the duration of the festival, sees nothing and only comes up for air when there is a problem. And he loves his job.

V FESTIVAL TODAY

The 2014 edition saw a few changes behind the scenes with Live Nation, a live event company based in California which promotes or produces over 22,000 events a year, becoming a majority shareholder and MTV taking over the broadcasting responsibilities from Channel 4. V has always been a well-oiled machine, however, and you cannot fault it for its organisation. It attracts more than 90,000 to the Weston Park site and about 180,000 to Chelmsford. In terms of the site, it's a pretty straight forward set-up at V: as well as the Virgin Media Stage, MTV Stage (previously the

NME Stage and 4Music Stage) Arena Stage, and Futures Stage, there is the recently re-named Glee Comedy Tent which has seen the likes of Kevin Bridges, Alan Carr, Katherine Ryan, Suzi Ruffell, Adam Hills, Andrew Bird, Tim Minchin and Sean Lock generate a giggle.

Camping is separate to the arena which means that when the performances finish across the stages in the main site you can head back to your campsite to partake in the apres-festival delicacies of a silent disco, fun fair or even snuggle down to watch a film. Like most festivals today alternative accommodation is available in the form of 'luxury' camping options, such as yurts, wooden cabins, gypsy caravans or camper vans (although this is pretty bog standard for any festival today).

The look on Gary Lightbody's face says it all realy... Snow Patrol take to the stage for another storming festival set.

WHO ATTENDS V?

For many V is not only their first time at a festival but also probably the first time they've ever erected a tent. But fear not, this is the best place to be if you have no idea what to do with a tent peg! You can always hire out a yurt, and there are hundreds of really friendly stewards who are more than happy to show you how it's done. In fact V is one of the friendliest festivals going. It has to be with its strict age policy. Under-16s must be accompanied by an over-18 adult and under 5s are not permitted.

V, first and foremost, is a hits festival and there aren't many bands who would attempt to be experimental or focus on those obscure B-sides during their set. This is reflected in the crowd who are not there to be impressed or to pick up anything new: they go knowing what they like and what they want to see and do. As a result there is a huge amount of cynicism from people towards V: I saw one particularly catty website describe V as a, 'music festival for people that don't actually like music but still want to say they have been to a festival.' Yes it's a pop gig environment and yes you are very likely to see cast members from *The Only Way Is Essex* (it hurts to even

'V FESTIVAL IS A REAL FESTIVAL FOR MUSIC LOVERS FROM ALL WALKS OF LIFE.'

write that) and *Hollyoaks*. But who are you or I to make a judgement on people and put some kind of level on music tastes? Some of the best acts in the business make a point of playing V; it's a real stalwart of the festival calendar and pop, rock and indie acts from across the board make sure they pass through the sultry fields of Weston Park to greet the V crowd with a tune or two. V always has a premier line-up and if you don't like Olly Murs or The Saturdays then V simply isn't the festival for you.

Right: Tom Meighan from Kasabian struts around the main stage at V.

Scan here to listen to Kasabian's reflections on their festival experience and how it's all about winning the crowd over.

THE MUSIC

A festival isn't complete without an appearance from Elbow. Here they are performing at a gorgeous night at V.

ELBOW

V Festival is a festival for real music lovers from all walks of life and this has been comprehensively backed up by the names that have already played it over the years – big names from around the world with a massive dose of pop, and a smidgen of an edge smothered in dance. When it started it was definitely more of a Brit pop and indie-based festival, but that has changed over the years to steer it even more towards the mainstream. You don't really go to V to discover new music; it's all very familiar and obvious. Coldplay, Muse, Oasis, Radiohead, Morrissey, Faithless, Tinie Tempah, Beyoncé, Kings of Leon, Kendrick Lamar, Rita Ora, Elbow, and Sam Smith have all played recent editions of the festival. In fact V has become a barometer of British pop over the years, with performers across all stages regularly reflecting the current trends in the music industry year on year.

The festival used to run a hugely successful competition called 'Road To V' through Channel 4's music strand, 4Music – a search for a couple of suitable unsigned acts to open the festival, with the final

choice decided on a public vote. Previous winners have included The Young Knives, The Last Republic and Bombay Bicycle Club, who were the final band to win the competition before it was scrapped. They joined a splendid roster of performers who have appeared over the years: from The Chemical Brothers to Olly Murs, and The Jesus and Mary Chain to Rizzle Kicks.

Liam Gallagher has been a regular at V, not just performing with Oasis and Beady Eye, but over the years he's been to watch All Saints, Paul Weller, Zutons, Ian Brown, Kasabian and The Prodigy. A real fan of the festival set-up, when talking to him back in 2005 ahead of Oasis' headline set, he appreciated that festivals allowed him to get out of the Oasis bubble and offered the band a different opportunity and outlet with less pressure than some of their regular shows. Plus he loves to get out and watch bands. For someone like Pixie Lott, a Chelmsford local, V is a great chance to check out the live music scene. She's been going to V since she was 15 and has camped every year, even when she's not playing.

V AND ME

I would not be able to tell you how many times I've been to the V Festival. I've worked at V, covering it for MTV and Channel 4 over the years; I've also lost a day or two of my life at V from forgetting my number one rule for attending a festival… 'pace yourself!' I have also been able to see some incredible performances, not least The Verve in 1998, the same year I saw them play Haigh Hall in Wigan.

The Chelmsford site and its close proximity to London makes it seem like an easy visit and it is one that I've done regularly. I've also been up to the Staffordshire site, mainly tagging along with my other half and the other Editors as they played over the years. On one particular occasion I didn't leave the Portakabin-style dressing room as the rain was so torrential and the hangover wouldn't have coped. What a waste! The more involving and earnest experience was when Kasabian headlined the 2nd stage in 2007 and I watched them completely hustle the crowd into one enormous trance-like state, with each and every one of them holding onto Tom Meighan's every word. It must have been a good 30 minutes after the band had left the stage that the audience were still chanting the melody to 'L.S.F' as if was some homing beacon to get them back to their tents and cars safely.

In 1998 I was covering V for MTV with a host of my fellow VJ's. At one particular moment June Sarpong and I were sent backstage to a secret Winnebago to interview the living legend James Brown. I was utterly terrified and had no idea what to expect once we opened that door. What we found was the Godfather of Soul suited and booted in his bright red velvet suit and Cuban heels, barking out those words and phrases he's known for the world over. What was more confusing and just odd was his manager/bodyguard walking around the entire time with a suitcase handcuffed to his wrist. It was money, apparently; he insisted on being paid in cash. Nice gig if you can get it. Local heroes The Prodigy have also been regulars at V Festival. But

'WHEN IT STARTED IT WAS DEFINITELY MORE A BRIT POP AND INDIE-BASED FESTIVAL, BUT THAT HAS CHANGED OVER THE YEARS TO STEER IT EVEN MORE TOWARDS THE MAINSTREAM.'

I've never managed to get back to one of their infamous parties...

V has also had its fair share of bands failing to play either due to 'illness' or contract issues. In 2009 Oasis managed to play the first day in Staffordshire but failed to make it through to day one in Chelmsford due to illness. The job of filling those boots was given to Snow Patrol – a slot that was only confirmed in the early afternoon as they arrived onsite. I watched as Snow Patrol more than satisfied that huge crowd in front of the main stage, who very nearly forgot all about Oasis' last minute change of plans. Although this wasn't a wholly new experience for Snow Patrol: they almost had to do the same thing the month before at T in the Park, not knowing as they went on stage if they would be required to replace the headliners or fulfil their booking as second to top. In the end they played a longer set at T until Blur arrived late to the site but made it on stage to headline. I think Gary Lightbody was more nervous the previous day when he joined headliner Deus on stage to sing 'Hotel Lounge' from their album *Worst Case Scenario* – an album that had very significant and lasting memories for him. It was one of the first albums Gary bought upon leaving home to move to Dundee to attend university and form Snow Patrol.

But my favourite memory occurred in 2013 when I was working for Channel 4. It was about 3pm on a blistering Saturday afternoon and I was waiting for Rudimental to come off stage to have a chat with them. Looking out from the side of stage, I'd never seen a crowd that excited or enormous – it looked like every single person on site was in front of that stage, aptly losing their minds to 'Feel The Love'. When they came off stage, the band told me it was the gig of their lives, having never experienced anything like it or seen that many people watch them before – and this from a band who had only, up to that point, played a handful of gigs over the course of a year. It was exhilarating to watch and emotional to behold. There was something about seeing that many people in the sunshine having the time of their life

'WITH V YOU CAN REALLY PLAN YOUR WEEKEND – YOU KNOW THE BANDS, YOU KNOW THE MUSIC AND YOU KNOW WHAT KIND OF EXPERIENCE YOU'RE GOING TO HAVE!'

and having an experience like that to live music. It reminds me of why I love what I do and why V Festival is indeed one of the biggest draws on the music festival calendar.

A GREAT FESTIVAL

I've always had a fun time at V. I've gone knowing who is playing and knowing who I will watch. I guess that's one of the main differences between V and many other festivals: with V you can really plan your weekend – you know the bands, you know the music and you know what kind of experience you're going to have. You are never going to stretch your musical muscle or discover some obscure cultural piece of performance art that will change your outlook on life. What you will do is have a great time with your mates, listening to the bands and artists you hear all the time on the radio and maybe see a member of *Hollyoaks* in the process.

Bestival's own caped-crusader Rudy enjoys his first ever festival experience!

WHERE: *Isle of Wight*   **WHEN:** *Mid September*

BESTIVAL
Most likely to see:
A giant, inflatable Lionel Richie head.

Scan here to see Edith's
Bestival essentials.

HISTORY: FROM SUNDAY BEST TO SUNDAY BESTIVAL

If I were to describe Bestival in a short sharp decree, I would say it's like being at one of your best mate's house parties. You know, the friend that's much cooler than they realise they are, effortlessly ahead of the game and making everyone feel alive and happy. That, for me, is the atmosphere of Bestival. And that atmosphere is without a shadow of a doubt down to Rob Da Bank, his wife Josie and the team behind Bestival.

Bestival began life in 2004 as a magical escape in Robin Country Park on the Isle of Wight. The brainchild of Rob Da Bank and his team, the seed of the festival was planted at the start of the millennium and grew from the success of the 'Sunday Best' parties held in London for the record label of the same name. The parties were the blueprints for the festival, maintaining the idea of 'punching above your weight, musically' and

Above: Everyone LOVES Bestival!

incorporating big headliners such as Fatboy Slim or Groove Armada into small venues. The idea of fun – not trendy – party people, with a hedonistic outlook, carried over from those parties and into a field in the Isle of Wight, after Rob and his team charmed the owners of the quaint adventure park, Robin Country Park. The festival, as a result, is all about good music for good people.

According to Rob the festival was 'surprisingly easy to get off the ground, as it felt like it had only been six months previous we were talking about it in the pub before the gates for the first one were opening. We made it happen on a shoe string and if we were doing it now I don't know if I would have the courage and the determination – let alone get the lending to get it off the ground.'

Rob Da Bank and his wife Josie, their business partners John and Ziggy, and manager Dan Turner all take the reigns across different areas of the festival. Rob, as you would expect, is in charge of music and

> **'IT TAKES A CONCERTED EFFORT TO REMAIN DIFFERENT AND STAND OUT FROM THE CROWD.'**

bookings; Josie is the creative mind of the festival as well as handling the day to day running; John looks after finance and ticketing; and Ziggy, John's partner, oversees marketing and sponsorship. There has always been a real 'family DIY' ethic at Bestival and it is something the organisers would like to maintain going forward.

Back in 2004 they started with an audience of just 4,000 people – a capacity which pretty much doubled every two years from then on in. In 2010, when they reached the enormous number of 55,000 music fans, they felt they had definitely reached a point they didn't want to surpass. That culminated in the organisers scaling back to 50,000. This was for a number of reasons: one was to allow the festival to survive a growing and demanding market, but it was also to keep the Bestival spirit prosperous and distinctive.

BESTIVAL TODAY

Bestival takes place in September and remains 100 per cent independent. Offers to sell-off areas of the festival have, of course, been made to the Da Banks and their team over the years, but Bestival is a labour of love and its organisers have clearly had its unique and special character at heart when considering any offers to take in external funding. What's more, Bestival is a member of the Association of Independent Festivals (AIF,) a non-profit trade association created by Rob Da Bank and Ben Turner to represent and empower independent UK music festivals.

From Belladrum to Open House, Eden Sessions to Village Green, and every other independent music festival that qualifies within the British Isles – they all benefit from the help, advice and support of this important organisation.

It takes a concerted effort to remain different and stand out from the crowd. But how do they go about remaining so unique? 'The fancy dress was and still is a great calling card,' says Rob. 'From that point on, though, we had to introduce new things. The mirror ball in 2014 was a huge talking point; it had a

Below: 2014's mirror ball was a closely guarded secret!

life of its own almost like a fourth headliner. Not only breaking a world record for the largest mirror ball in the world, but almost like an art installation – people would make a point of getting their picture beside it or just making time to go and visit it. Similarly in 2013, where else would you get the opportunity to go inside a giant inflatable Lionel Richie head?'

Indeed, it's the one-off experiences you wouldn't get anywhere else – from the Women's Institute Tea Tent to The Port – they all provide their own idiosyncratic experiences. In the same way that conceptual artist Jeremy Deller would encourage pop art to be shown in less conventional locations, Rob Da Bank sometimes thinks of the festival as a huge art installation.

PEOPLE AND PLANNING

There is definitely a direct link between the type of crowd at Bestival today and the type of crowd that turned up at the Clapham tearoom for the Sunday Best parties in the late 1990s. Attending Bestival is about having an open mind; it's also about having no expectation apart from the want to have a good time and the idea that nothing can ruin the joy of being amongst like-minded people who love music. They're a group of people looking for a utopia – a magical experience and pure escapism – leaving their mundane and everyday lives behind to be someone else for the weekend. And for some it really does provide them

with a life-changing experience. It's also about escape, and the effort required to get there; crossing a sea makes it feel like it's a holiday or a getaway. This is the essence of the spirit of Bestival – just spend five minutes in front of the Port stage and you will instantly feel the energy of the festival and a sharp realisation of what is expected of you and what you can expect over the weekend.

Getting to Bestival requires a certain amount of planning and consideration, and you are more than likely to bump into at least one band or artist on the ferry over to the Isle of Wight. Go by foot and take the shuttle bus onto site, or take your own vehicle across and take advantage of your surroundings to explore the island. Either that or you could swim across! Speaking of which, there is a charity event, Swim 2 Bestival, which began in 2007 by a group of university mates after they became bored of queuing for the ferry. Now an annual event which allows festival goers to swim the 1.3 mile stretch across the Solent for charity, it has raised over £40,000 for good causes and allowed over 100 swimmers to cross one of the busiest shipping lanes in Europe. That, to me, is an example of the upmost dedication in getting to a festival; in fact it might be the most impressive arrival at a festival ever.

THE MUSIC

The best way to describe the music at Bestival is to think of it as a jukebox. I know jukeboxes are a little outdated but there is a bar in Glasgow called 'Nice n' Sleazys' and it still has the best jukebox in the world! It has tons of songs and artists you love and loads of things you didn't even know you loved. But it's the feeling of being in that room with friends and having a shared experience, which brings those songs, from whatever era, from whatever genre, to life at that particular moment. That, to me, is what a Bestival line-up offers: it's the best party soundtrack you will ever hear from new and old, disco to rap, indie to world music – it's all in there along with everything else. And even if you come across something that you thought you weren't into, by the time you've watched the set with whoever you are with or even if you just catch one song, it all adds up to the musical jigsaw that is your Bestival experience.

Bestival always has a theme, and dressing up and escapism has always been a huge part of the festival. The theme doesn't necessarily tie in with the main acts; sometimes it does, sometimes not. The Desert Island Disco theme of 2014 proved extremely popular and saw a large number of artists embrace the theme on stage in both their production and in their song choices. The organisers normally know what the theme is first before any bands are booked, although not every band fits into that particular theme. Booking bands for any festival – let alone one with a theme – must be a testing procedure. 'It can be quite a nail-biting time and it has its ups and downs,' says Rob da Bank. For example, 2013's headliner Elton John confirmed a whole year in advance, allowing Rob to put his feet up for the rest of the year! On the flip side Rob could be in February with no headliners confirmed and that then bleeds into ticket sales and interest in the festival. As Rob says: 'if you announce a shit line-up then it's not going to sell you 50,000 tickets. They love Bestival; they know they are going to have a great time but you still have to deliver on the top line.'

Rob da Bank and his Bestival cohorts were kind of seen as the 'Golden Children' of the festival

'IT'S THE BEST PARTY SOUNDTRACK YOU WILL EVER HEAR FROM NEW AND OLD, DISCO TO RAP, AND INDIE TO WORLD MUSIC.'

circuit in their first three years due to an outstanding line-up that included Fatboy Slim, Lee 'Scratch' Perry, Super Furry Animals, 2manydjs, Pet Shop Boys, Scissor Sisters, Hot Chip and John Martyn, amongst hundreds of others. Now it's all about maintaining the quality, but with the likes of Outkast, Beck, Chic and Foals headlining the 2014 edition, it seems as if Rob et al are already upping their game.

BESTIVAL AND ME

Scan here to listen to Bobby Gillespie talk about performing at a festival.

Bestival is one of my absolute favourite festivals and having been lucky enough to know and work with Rob, I can say honestly with my hand on my heart that the festival is an extension of his wonderful personality and hospitality, and more than that – his absolute unconditional passion for music. I've had a few experiences at Bestival: I've lost myself with friends; I've DJ'd; I've been with friends who have played at the festival too. My most memorable experience, however, was taking my six-year-old son for his first Bestival experience. We went for the day in our disco capes, jumping on a train from London, catching a bus to the port then boat over to the island. It was an adventure in itself – our special mother-and-son-date weekend to share and sample sounds and sights together for the first time. The expression on my son's face as we made our way through the woods down towards the port – the bassline vibrating through the trees, the excitement in the air – it painted a permanent smile on his face. We flew around the site with our disco capes on; he laughed like I've never heard him laugh while watching The Cuban Brothers; we danced to Monki in the queue (five times) for the toboggan ride; we had our picture taken by the glitter ball; bought afro wigs; ate pizza; and watched the final ever Dan le Sac vs. Scroobius Pip gig. That particular performance demanded a pretty intense mum and son chat about language afterwards, which was quickly forgotten, thankfully. It was over too quick, if I'm being honest, so from that year on we go en masse with his mates to Camp Bestival…

CAMP BESTIVAL

'CAMP BESTIVAL IS LIKE THE KIDS' FIELD AT GLASTONBURY, BUT THE FORMER IS A WHOLE FESTIVAL WITH THAT ETHOS, CARE AND ATTENTION, FUN AND COLOUR.'

Everything I've said about Bestival could be said about Camp Bestival – the smaller sibling of Bestival, which is held at Lulworth Castle in Dorset in July and is primarily aimed at families with younger kids. With a capacity of 30,000 it still gives kids and their parents the chance to fully experience festival escapism with a mind-blowing line-up, which hits the spot musically but offers up those pretty special moments for kids to show the adults some cool stuff, in a role reversal way. You are not the one telling them they might like this or that – they are dragging you along to watch Mr Tumble or take part in the world record attempt for the most paper airplanes flying at once, or to watch *Shrek The Musical*. It's a beautiful and life-affirming experience for both parties. Camp Bestival is like the kids' field at Glastonbury, but the former is a whole festival with a particular ethos, care and attention, fun and colour.

Camp Bestival was born in 2008 after both Rob's wife, Josie, and his partner's wife, Ziggy, fell pregnant around the same time. They created it especially for children and now that Josie and Rob have three boys it was important for them to have somewhere they could take the children to enjoy the same things they love about being at festivals – but in a tailored environment, somewhere slightly mellower than Bestival, but which still provided a safe environment and fun experience. The mini-Bestival has certainly set the benchmark for family festivals, and what is extraordinarily brilliant is the opportunity to take your kids to a wonderful location such as Lulworth Castle and also being able to let your hair down. Bravo to that!

Camp Bestival is Bestival's enchanting younger sister and the perfect festival for the little ones.

Belle and Sebastian's Stuart Murdoch was the original mastermind of the Bowlie Weekender.

WHERE: *Various locations*   **WHEN:** *Various times during the year*

ALL TOMORROW'S PARTIES
Most likely to see: A suit-wearing theremin-playing
band member wandering around the fjords of Iceland.

Scan here to see Edith's
ATP essentials.

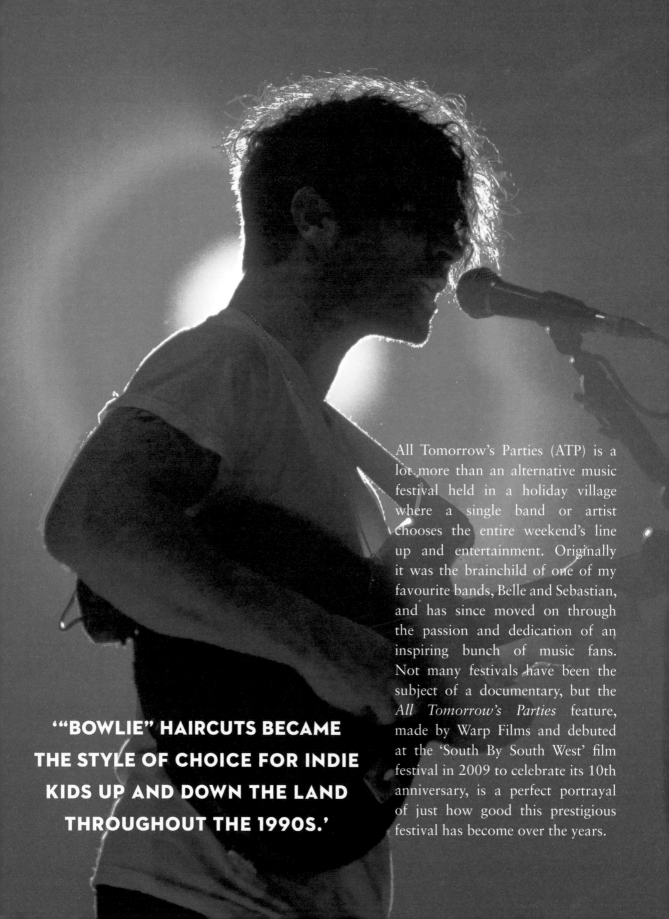

'"BOWLIE" HAIRCUTS BECAME THE STYLE OF CHOICE FOR INDIE KIDS UP AND DOWN THE LAND THROUGHOUT THE 1990S.'

All Tomorrow's Parties (ATP) is a lot more than an alternative music festival held in a holiday village where a single band or artist chooses the entire weekend's line up and entertainment. Originally it was the brainchild of one of my favourite bands, Belle and Sebastian, and has since moved on through the passion and dedication of an inspiring bunch of music fans. Not many festivals have been the subject of a documentary, but the *All Tomorrow's Parties* feature, made by Warp Films and debuted at the 'South By South West' film festival in 2009 to celebrate its 10th anniversary, is a perfect portrayal of just how good this prestigious festival has become over the years.

THE BOWLIE BOYS AND GIRLS...

But how did it all begin? We need to first look back at the Bowlie Weekender, named after the popular 1970s Glaswegian haircut, and an event organised and curated by Belle and Sebastian at the Pontin's holiday village in Camber Sands in April 1999. The band hand-picked all the music, which saw everyone from Snow Patrol to Mogwai, and Teenage Fanclub to Jarvis Cocker playing or DJing. It was a bit like having one of your favourite bands make a mix tape of their favourite music, but instead of playing the tape, everyone came along to play live! Belle and Sebastian's Stuart Murdoch had previously worked at a holiday village in Scotland when he was younger and it was from that experience, and his love and admiration of the legendary Northern Soul Weekenders (an exciting British cultural movement in its own right), that the idea for the festival was born.

Barry Hogan was the original booker at the Bowlie Weekender and went on to set up All Tomorrow's Parties, named after The Velvet Underground song. The original Bowlie festival gathered a cult following – with 'Bowlie' haircuts becoming the style of choice for indie kids up and down the land throughout the 1990s – and various up-and-coming bands were eager to play at the festival. Stuart Braithwaite from Mogwai played the first Bowlie Weekender after they heard about the event and asked to play, and were paid in tickets for the festival. They then went on to help Barry Hogan curate All Tomorrow's Parties in its first year; this involved sending Barry a list of the band's favourite artists and it was down to Barry to see who he could get within the budget. Mogwai's list included Sigur Rós who played for £500 back then!

'Everything appealed to us,' Barry Hogan recalls about the first few years of the festival. 'The experience of choosing the bands as well as the chance to play to a lot of like-minded music fans. It's that lovely idea that a band who loves music might pick artists who they have listened to for years but never had the chance to see live, and by booking them on their very own curated weekend might be the first time they see them along with their own fans. What a wonderful experience to be part of.'

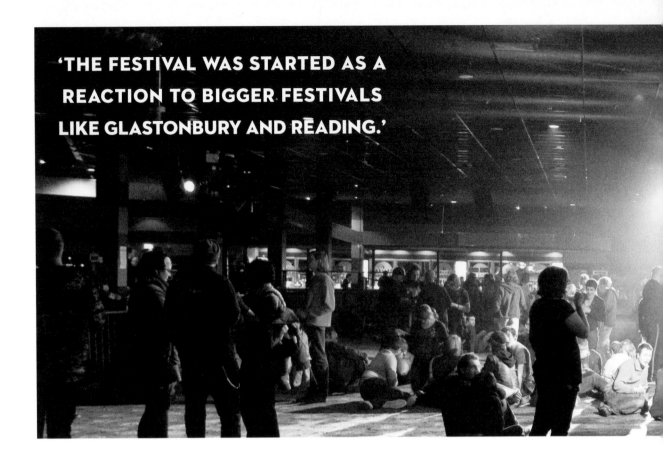

'THE FESTIVAL WAS STARTED AS A REACTION TO BIGGER FESTIVALS LIKE GLASTONBURY AND READING.'

Before long, the Bowlie Weekender spawned All Tomorrow's Parties, which then went on to hold a similarly curated event in the same location, moving in 2006 from Camber Sands to Butlins in Minehead. What's more, a record label and promotion company was formed under the All Tomorrow's Parties moniker with a view to promoting and signing-up bands with close links to the festival.

The festival was started as a reaction to bigger festivals such as Glastonbury and Reading where acts like Tortoise or Smog either weren't considered for the line-up or weren't given the appropriate environment to be seen. Keep in mind this was

before Green Man, Field Day, End of The Road and Bestival, all of which were directly or indirectly influenced by the All Tomorrow's Parties set-up. In fact the festival's organisers' raison d'être was essentially to provide an alternative and progressive music festival with a line-up that really pushed boundaries in an environment that artists and fans were treated with respect – which is something the aforementioned festivals could certainly get on board with. What's more, the curators not only picked the line-up but also programmed the schedule on 'ATP TV'. Each chalet has a television that shows curated material from the festival, so even if

Above: The crowd chills out at Butlins ahead of another glorious ATP performance.

'THE FESTIVAL IS ALL ABOUT NEW, FRESH AND PROGRESSIVE MUSIC.'

you want a break from the music, you are still absorbing something tied in with the essence of ATP – might that be a film, a video or even a poetry reading.

The holiday village environment is another thing that sets ATP out from the rest – a setting that is also a complete polar opposite of the audience it attracts. Watching the original *All Tomorrow's Parties* Warp feature, you'll see the same environment back in the 1970s, with people dancing, running around in the sunshine, playing on the beach with an air of disregard for the outside world – basically having the archetypal British holiday. I guess the location fitted in perfectly with the whole Belle and Sebastian image, that kitch, retro spirit. It couldn't have been more ideal really. The setting also offers a fantastically fun place to spend a weekend listening to music and hanging out with mates. I grew up in a little fishing village where nothing was more exciting than when the fairground rolled into town every summer, where you'd spend hours in the arcade or being sick on the waltzers. That's the same way I feel about ATP – that feeling of whiling away your school holidays, checking out bands, chilling out with your mates in one of the kitch Butlins chalets – it's a nostalgic journey.

ATP TODAY

ATP is always exploring ways of presenting new events in unique and unusual locations, and they were fortunate that due to the immediate success of the festival they were able to expand the brand worldwide. Iceland, Australia, America and Barcelona have all played host to ATP events, the latter of which has close links between ATP and Primavera Sound. Sometimes, however, the idea of a curator can get lost in translation and although the events were a tremendous experience, it can be hard to make the numbers work financially. I asked my very dear friend the broadcaster and author Douglas Anderson, who has made films with Belle and Sebastian and been to ATP on numerous occasions, whether he thought ATP was an important festival: 'Any festival is important if it caters for your artistic desires, but I think ATP is important due to the fact that there are artists curating and giving both well- and lesser-known artists the chance to play alongside each other on the same bill.' Indeed Barry Hogan also encourages non-music curators and has one person in particular he would love to collaborate with in the future: Wes Anderson. A film-maker, music lover and all round auteur, the Texan director would indeed be a wonderful curator for what is a truly original festival.

Unusually the festival has never had sponsorship – a rarity that Barry Hogan appreciates when looking back at the festival's origins: '[sponsorship] was possible but unfortunately less and less so as we go along where we are competing against so many other festivals. We are now totally open to sponsorship in the right way and hope we can achieve it in a way that remains true to our original ethos. We now see sponsorship and grants as a way to help make the events a better experience for the artists and fans alike.' I imagine that is a very tough call to make but I know from a fans' point of view sponsorship allows the festival to survive for many years to come, and I would much rather that than not at all.

Warren Ellis
performs at ATP.

THE MUSIC

All Tomorrow's Parties, as the name suggests, is all about new, fresh and progressive music. When I asked Barry Hogan about their output and if he could describe the type of music heard at the festival he simply said, 'good music.' What a simple and precise objective! But I guess it comes down to who the festival chooses as its curator – whether they are a performer or a music lover. In the 50 plus festivals that ATP have run, everyone from Sonic Youth, to Portishead, and Jim Jarmusch to *The Simpsons* creator Matt Groening, have curated a weekend. For organiser Barry Hogan, one of the most memorable collaborations was working with Dirty Three in 2007, the experimental Australian trio set up by Warren Ellis, erstwhile 'Bad Seed' and long time Nick Cave collaborator. 'Working with those guys was a pure inspiration and their zest for developing an incredible line-up was inspiring,' says Hogan. 'We have become close friends since that collaboration.'

If you get the chance to watch the fantastic Warp Films documentary on the festival you can see Warren's passion for the festival; he spends most of the time watching other bands, enjoying the music and hanging out with fans. Nick Cave's band Grinderman also played the 2007 edition and when asked his opinion of the festival and what was on offer, Cave described it as 'being spoilt with riches.' Since the curator chooses the music, it's not

'ALL TOMORROW'S PARTIES WAS AN INSTANT SUCCESS WHEN IT STARTED BECAUSE THERE REALLY WASN'T ANYTHING QUITE LIKE IT.'

about trends and what's popular at the time or going to be popular, it reflects the world of the artist. Each curator has his or her own tastes and interests and does not necessarily aim for particular genres; it could be anything from bands such as The Octopus Project and Lightning Bolt.

ALL TOMORROW'S PEOPLE...

'This is an experience for music fans and people with a very broad taste in quality music who like everything from Aphex Twin to Vashti Bunyan or GZA,' says organiser Barry Hogan. Traditionally the festival has had no separation between fans and bands; everyone mixes and socialises in the same environment so there are no VIP bars or segregation. And because of that it seemed like a natural development to allow the fans to decide on the line-up and curate their own festival – something that actually materialised when the fans curated their own edition in 2007 (put together by a poll collated via the chalets of every paying guest!).

All Tomorrow's Parties was an instant success when it started because there really wasn't anything quite like it. From my own point of view it was a real breath of fresh air and I found the personal choices made by some of my favourite musicians a real draw – like being invited to my own private viewing of their record collection. It was the start of the boutique festival, a collection of alternative music acts in one place with an emphasis on intimacy and equality for fans and musicians. Fans go for the music, for the band that has curated the event and for the bands they have chosen. It's also a welcome retreat from the normal festival environment, thanks to the holiday park set-up which means no camping! Instead you get a bed, warm showers, a specially programmed TV and a self-catering chalet that you can use as you wish (maybe to have people around for a post-headliner-debriefing-dinner or maybe to hold your own impromptu gig!). Anything is possible and anything is encouraged. The audience is a real mix of those who have been before along with young music fans who are determined to stretch their palate and explore what's available. There is an element of trust from people, as well as respect. It's not about being a music snob; All Tomorrow's Parties is cultivated by people who know what they are doing, both in the artists curating and the organisers putting it all together.

'ANYTHING IS POSSIBLE AND ANYTHING IS ENCOURAGED.'

Scan here to listen to Damon Albarn's festival memories.

'FOR ALL TOMORROW'S PARTIES'

'And where will she go and what shall she do, when midnight comes around…' so sang Nico in the song that lends its name to the festival. And yet there is so much to explore at ATP, with endless opportunities to really open your mind and explore the boundaries of art and music. ATP really is like no other festival and that is down to a number of factors: firstly the location, which suits the whole atmosphere of the festival and offers an abundance of little satellite performances – whether that's in a chalet, an arcade or a bingo hall. Secondly a band or artist choosing the weekend's programme is such an appealing concept as a music fan. A line-up put together by a musician you admire, and then having the opportunity to step inside a world that is basically a physical mix tape made by them, is my idea of heaven. Being recommended music, art, film, poetry and other creative forms by one of your favourite bands is a very welcome alternative to more mainstream festivals that don't really have that intimacy. Sometimes the line-up at a festival can be safe and obvious, but I admire ATP and all it stands for, not least for its bravery and conviction.

MY FESTIVAL

JANUARY

EDINBURGH HOGMANAY
Where: Edinburgh
edinburghshogmanay.com/whats-on
…

THE GREAT BRITISH ROCK & BLUES FESTIVAL
Where: Skegness
bigweekends.com/the-weekends/specialist-music-weekends/great-british-rock-blues-festival.aspx
…

BRADFORD ROOTS FESTIVAL
Where: Bradford
wiltshiremusic.org.uk/whatson/brootswend

FEBRUARY

GIANTS OF ROCK
Where: Somerset
bigweekends.com/the-weekends/specialist-music-weekends/giants-of-rock.aspx
…

FOLK THREE
Where: Cheltenham
cheltenhamtownhall.org.uk
…

BBC RADIO 6 MUSIC FESTIVAL
Where: Various locations
bbc.co.uk/6music

MARCH

BRISTOL INTERNATIONAL JAZZ FESTIVAL
Where: Bristol
bristoljazzandbluesfest.com

THE 'BUGGED OUT' WEEKENDER
Where: Bognor Regis
buggedoutweekender.net

APRIL

LONDON INTERNATIONAL SKA FESTIVAL
Where: London
londoninternationalskafestival.co.uk
…

RESISTANZ FESTIVAL
Where: Sheffield
corporation.org.uk/resistanzfestival
…

MAY

WE ARE FSTVL
Where: London
wearefstvl.com
…

THE GREAT ESCAPE FESTIVAL
Where: Brigthon
greatescapefestival.com
…

RADIO 1'S BIG WEEKEND
Where: Various locations
bbc.co.uk/radio1/bigweekend
…

WYCHWOOD MUSIC FESTIVAL
Where: Cheltenham
wychwoodfestival.com

JUNE

FIELD DAY
Where: London
fielddayfestivals.com
…

PARKLIFE WEEKENDER
Where: Manchester
parklife.uk.com/lineup.php

ISLE OF WIGHT FESTIVAL
Where: Isle of Wight
isleofwightfestival.com
…

YEAR

You've got the guide, now it's time to plan your festival year! Here's a list of some of the best festivals taking place throughout the year around the UK and a link to further information (subject to change). Don't forget festivals constantly change their dates, so please check the website before you book anything. Have fun!

DOWNLOAD FESTIVAL
Where: Derbyshire
downloadfestival.co.uk
...

ROCKNESS
Where: Loch Ness, Scotland
rockness.co.uk
...

GLASTONBURY
Where: Somerset
glastonburyfestivals.co.uk

JULY

ALL TOMORROW'S PARTIES
Where: Various locations
atpfestival.com
...

LATITUDE
Where: Suffolk
latitudefestival.com
...

T IN THE PARK
Where: Perthshire, Scotland
tinthepark.com
...

HOP FARM
Where: Hop Farm, Kent
thehopfarmmusicfestival.com

AUGUST

GREEN MAN
Where: Brecon Beacons, Wales
greenman.net
...

READING AND LEEDS
Where: Reading and Leeds
readingfestival.com
...

V FESTIVAL
Where: Chelmsford and Staffordshire
vfestival.com
...

WILDERNESS FESTIVAL
Where: Oxford
wildernessfestival.com

SEPTEMBER

FESTIVAL NO. 6
Where: Portmeirion, Wales
festivalnumber6.com
...

BESTIVAL
Where: Isle of Wight
bestival.net

OCTOBER

MUSICPORT FESTIVAL
Where: Whitby
musicportfestival.com
...

GLASTONBURY TICKET REGISTRATION OPENS!

NOVEMBER

HARD ROCK HELL FESTIVAL
Where: North Wales
hardrockhell.com
...

KEEP YOUR EYES PEELED FOR 'EARLY BIRD' TICKETS, WHICH NORMALLY GO ON SALE DURING THE AUTUMN MONTHS!

DECEMBER

GLASTONBURY HEADLINERS ANNOUNCED!
...

ALSO KEEP A LOOK OUT FOR THE OCCASIONAL ALL TOMORROW'S PARTIES 'WINTER' EDITION!

LIST OF PHOTOGRAPHS